Andrzej Marczewski

EVEN NINJA MONKEYS LIKE TO PLAY

UNICORN EDITION

Gamification, Game Thinking and Motivational Design

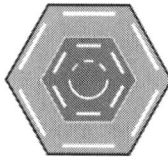

Gamified UK

Even Ninja Monkeys Like to Play: Unicorn Edition

© 2018 Andrzej Marczewski

Gamified UK

www.gamified.uk

@daverage

Originally edited by Dutch Driver http://www.choragus.co/

& Laura Marczewski

User Type and Mechanic Icons, where not custom drawn, are under the CC3 License and downloaded from www.game-icons.net

Figure 32 Oxytocin "Oxytocin with labels" by Edgar181 - Own work. Licensed under Public Domain via Wikimedia Commons - https://commons.wiki-media.org/wiki/File:Oxytocin_with_labels.png#/media/File:Oxytocin_with_la-bels.png

ISBN: 9781724017109

10 9 8 7 6 5 4 3

Originally this was dedicated to just my Mother who passed in 2007. I dedicate this version to both my Mum and my Dad (who is still alive and well!).

Both encouraged me and believed in myself when many would not early in my life.

It is thanks in large part to them that I am who I am today.

CONTENTS

ACKNOWLEDGEMENTS

First, I want to thank my wife and wonderful family. Without their support and understanding, I would never have had the confidence or the strength to pursue my interests in gamification. Without my kids, I would not have half of the insights into games and play that I have now!

I also want to say thanks to the whole of the gamification community. It is a small community filled with amazing and generous people. I would like to thank Professor Richard Bartle, who has always provided great feedback on my work when asked and who helped immensely during the early phases of creating my User Types. Next, Roman Rackwitz, who is my gamification muse and Marigo Raftopoulos, another amazing sounding board for ideas in gamification.

I want to thank the great people who read draughts of the book and gave valuable feedback. Mike Finney, Richard Wallace, Kevin Werbach, Rob Alvarez Bucholska and Karl Kapp to name just a few.

Penultimately, all those who bought the first edition and still went out and got this one, you are awesome, and I love you!

Finally, huge thanks to Dutch Driver, another expert in the field of gamification, for his Herculean efforts to edit the original book, despite my best attempts to get in his way.

INTRODUCTION

I have always been a gamer. One of my earliest memories is of playing games on the Apple II that my Dad had borrowed from work, *Star Trek* I believe. Since then, games have always been a big part of my life. From my Commodore 64, through to the SNES then LAN gaming at friends' houses on *Duke Nuke'em* and *Doom*.

At university, I discovered the joys of *clan*-based gaming when I joined the Elites of Starship Troopers playing *Starship Troopers: Battlespace* on the AOL network [1]. This led me to start my own clan, Rages Renegades. Those years were important to me in ways I could never have realised!

In 2006, I started Yet Another Review Site [2] to write about games. By then I had been a web designer for six years, been involved in creating interactive learning materials and had formed a love for all thing's technology related.

In 2012, these interests all seemed to collide when I discovered gamification. It was like a lightning bolt hitting me. All my thoughts on how important games could be to people, from learning to social good – were all catered for in gamification. I started to blog about it obsessively, learning everything I could about the topic. I released a book [3] in the same year and started to get involved in speaking and consulting on the topic.

What you have in your hands now is a kind of reboot of that original book, in fact, it is the second edition of that reboot (a reboot of a reboot???) Based on my blogs over the last few years as well as essays and articles, some of the content follows a similar theme to the original books, a lot of it is different, new or evolved – it is certainly better written and edited. Look at it as the Ultimate Edition with all of the DLC and patches added on.

It will take you on a journey through the theory behind games and play, into the more practical realms of designing gamified solutions, all through my eyes.

My hope is that this book will equip you with enough information to feel confident enough to speak about gamification and start using it for your own projects.

A quick note on the title. I went through many iterations of the title. I went on Google+, Facebook, Twitter and more asking for advice. Then my daughter made an amazing comment. *"Daddy, when I grow up I want to be a ninja or a unicorn with wings called Princess Unicorn."*

Then it struck me. It didn't really matter what the title was, so I tried to think of the coolest thing I could. Who doesn't love monkeys or ninjas? With this second edition, I was even able to include the unicorns! In fact, I nearly called this version "Even Unicorns Dream of Flying?" So, equipped with that insight into my mind, read on, enjoy and remember – even ninja monkeys (or unicorns) like to play!

So much has changed since the first edition. After the book was finished, I took my Master on holiday – despite his insistence that I kidnapped him. He soon went mad, talking about creating a new edition of the book. That was when we met our new friend, Rainbow Unicorn. New or heavily updated content will be highlighted by Rainbow for you with a unicorn!

THE THEORY OF GAMES, PLAY AND

GAMIFICATION

What is Gamification?

This chapter will show you some of the history of the word gamification as well as a few definitions. My Master's definition is also there for you to ~~laugh~~ look at.

Every story needs to have a beginning, and this is no different.

ONCE UPON A TIME, in 2002, Nick Pelling officially coined a word (at least that is the version I know) [4]. That word is the whole reason you are now reading this book. The word was *gamification*. Nick had a vision. He wanted to make non-game related interfaces, such as cash machines (ATM's), more like games. In his word's gamification was:

> *"Applying game-like accelerated user interface design to make electronic transactions both enjoyable and fast"*

Sadly, his dreams never came to fruition; he was ahead of his time. In fact, it was not until 2010 that it really started to appear in common usage. Since then the definition of gamification has evolved, in terms of both wording and meaning. Wikipedia's history of definitions is quite interesting (to gamification geeks like me at least!) [5].

Before I offer my own definition of gamification, it is worth quoting the ones you are likely to see most often. First up is Sebastian Deterding's definition [6], *"The use of game design elements in non-game contexts,"* which is the most widely recognised.

Another one that has gained popularity is Kevin Werbach's [7] *"The process of making activities more game-like,"* which is my personal favourite from other experts.

My definition, when cornered, is;

"The use of game design metaphors to create more game-like and engaging experiences".

The reason for this will become clear over the course of the book; however, here is a quick breakdown of its meaning.

Game Design Metaphors: Lessons, elements and strategies from games and game design applied to non-game contexts.

Game-Like: The use of these metaphors to create experiences that feel related to games, without being games.

Engaging Experiences: This is the key to gamification, engagement. I define engagement as active, focused and intrinsically motivated participation. Therefore, with gamification, we are trying to create experiences that promote this.

At times, you will be asked to give a simple definition for people who really do not get all the fuss about games. I find the following quite helpful;

"The use of concepts and elements that make games engaging and enjoyable, in other areas of work or life in general".

Do not be afraid of the word gamification. It has a bad reputation at times, but that does not mean you should not use it. Some will tell you that you should speak about "Behavioural Change" or "Human Centric Design", and I have been guilty of this myself.

However, you are better off getting a good understanding of what gamification really is (by reading this book of course...) and then be able to stand your ground with compelling reasons why gamification is so great!

Something that is vital to say here is that gamification is **not** the process of making **games**! I will go into much more detail later, but just keep that in mind. We are not trying to make *Super Mario Excel or Call of Word 2013*! In fact, Raph Koster made a wonderful statement on his blog whilst I was writing this, that I think is very relevant here:

> *"UX design is about removing problems from the user.*
> *Game design is about giving problems to the user."*

If you consider that gamification is a form of user experience (UX) design, you can see just how different the two really are.

What Are Games and Play?

As the title suggests, I love to play. Sadly, my Master is not as fun as he makes out. It has been so long since I last played, I have almost forgotten how. This chapter is my favourite as it reminds me of what play is all about.

Defining Play

There are many definitions of play that people with an interest probably argue over! The most well know is that of Johan Huizinga from his book Homo Ludens. He describes play in the following way.

"Summing up the formal characteristic of play, we might call it a free activity standing quite consciously outside 'ordinary' life as being 'not serious' but at the same time absorbing the player intensely and utterly. It is an activity connected with no material interest, and no profit can be gained by it. It proceeds within its own proper boundaries of time and space according to fixed rules and in an orderly manner. It promotes the formation of social groupings that tend to surround themselves with secrecy and to stress the difference from the common world by disguise or other means. [8]*"*

Mine is a little less complex and fits with my personal philosophies on play.

Play is a free-form activity that is undertaken because it brings fun or joy.

The nature of play helps us to understand the building blocks of games. The rest of this chapter will go into this in much more detail, suffice to say – it really is not as simple as it seems, but it is fascinating!

Lusory Attitude

Play has been an area of academic study since the times of Plato! Whilst I researched play, one word became hard to ignore - ludic.

It comes up often in papers and articles about play. Ludic is derived from the Latin for play, *ludus*, and is defined as *"Showing spontaneous and undirected playfulness"* [9].

Ludic turns up in various forms when academics speak about play. Here are a few examples.

- **Ludus**: the original Latin for play
- **Ludeme**: an element or unit of play [10]
- **Prelusory goals**: goals set by the game
- **Lusory means**: rules set by the game
- **Lusory attitude**: a playful mindset, an understanding that you are entering play

The last three are from Bernard Suit's definition of a game described in his seminal book *The Grasshopper: Games, Life and Utopia* [10].

> *"To play a game is to attempt to achieve a specific state of affairs [prelusory goal], using only means permitted by rules [lusory means], where the rules prohibit use of more efficient in favour of less efficient means [constitutive rules], and where the rules are accepted just because they make possible such activity [lusory attitude]."*

This "lusory" attitude is the key that separates play from any other activity. As an example, read this passage as if it related to a job or academic studies.

- You start with a tutorial. It sets the context for what you are do-ing as well as giving you the basic skills to start.
- You are then given a set of tasks to complete and goals.
- Next, you start performing simple tasks repeatedly to improve your knowledge and skills.
- As your level of skill increases, new challenges become available and new goals are set. These require you to learn new skills and increase your abilities.
- Along the way, there are surprises and unexpected events. You will meet new people; some will be friends who you will work with, some will not.
- All the while, you will be collecting experience and currency as you complete progress.

Now, read it with a lusory or playful attitude. Approach it as if you were reading about a new game.

Play, Toys and Games

All of this raises the question of what play is and how it is different from games.

Play

There are many views of play out there. My view is that play is a free-form activity that is undertaken because it brings fun and joy. In this sort of description, play is an activity – it follows a similar line of thought to that proposed by historian, Johan Huizinga in Homo Ludens [8].

Huizinga also gave us another important concept. When considering games and play, the *Magic Circle*. The Magic Circle can be visualised as a boundary between reality and play, with you sat at the centre of it as you play.

There are many variations on this idea, most famously Frames from Gregory Bateson [11] and its expansion by Erving Goffman. [12] This expansion described a frame as a set of unspoken, implicit rules that surround the fantasy world, created through play, referred to as meta-communication.

Play does not need to have a point or a defined goal to it. It exists within a set of rules created by the person or people playing and is born in the imagination. Often it is a way of exploring the boundaries and extremes of something.

Play is essential for children as it teaches them about their environment and themselves [13]. It is also important to consider that children play just because they can, and it entertains them! Like adults, they are seeking novel experiences.

When my daughters were very young, they used to engage in pure play. They did things because they were new and judging by their smiles and their laughter – they enjoyed it. I would go so far as to say they found it fun. Play did not need external objects at first; they could just move their foot and find that hilarious. As they developed, their own movements became less interesting, probably because they had discovered the boundaries of what could be done, so players needed to have some help. They would pick up props and use them in ways they found entertaining. These props became toys.

Toys

Toys are an interesting concept when considering games and play. In this context, toys are objects or representation of objects that have their own implicit rules but do not come with explicit rules as standard. Game designer Chris Crawford neatly describes the nature of toys in a series of dichotomies he created to define games [14].

"If no goals are associated with a plaything, it is a toy."

Examples would be a ball, a stick, a Transformer, etc. You can play with them in any manner you chose, confined only by the toy's own rules: effect of gravity, shape, fragility etc.

If you throw a ball, depending on the material the ball is made from, it might bounce, it might roll, or it might stop dead. These are not rules that the person playing imposes on the ball. If you throw a Transformer in the same way as a ball, it will obey its own rules. It will not bounce and will probably break when you throw it at a wall!

There is another type of toy worth mentioning – I refer to it as a playground or a toy box; often you will hear them called sandboxes. This is an entire environment rather than a single object. When you examine a game such as *Minecraft* in the creator mode, you are in a virtual world that has its own implicit rules for how the world behaves. This world has constraints that you as the player have to abide by.

How far you can dig down, how far you can build up, how certain blocks behave with other blocks and more.

However, within those constraints, you can do what you want. You can use the world itself as a toy and play with it. That can include turning the world into the setting for a game!

Going back to my daughter's experiences. At first, they would just play with the toys, they would not create any discernible rules around how they interacted with the toys. After a while, that was no longer enough. It was not fun just to throw bricks at the wall; they started to add rules to the play like stacking them as high as they could or lining up the colours. The free-form play now had structure – it had become a simple game.

Games

Like play, games have many, many definitions. To illustrate this, here are just a few!

"[...] a word like "game" points to a somewhat diffuse "system" of prototype frames, among which some frame-shifts are easy, but others involve more strain" [15]
Marvin Minsky

"The voluntary attempt to overcome unnecessary obstacles" [16]
Bernard Suits

"A series of meaningful choices" [17]
Sid Meier

"A game is a problem-solving activity, approached with a playful attitude." [18]
Jesse Schell

"A game is a system in which players engage in an artificial conflict, defined by rules, that results in a quantifiable outcome." [19]
Eric Zimmerman and Katie Salen

"A structured experience with rules and goals that is fun."
Amy Jo Kim

Simply put, play begins to become a game when you start to add explicit goals and impose system-based rules.

If I kick the ball through a goal, I get a point and I win (Zero sum). If we work together to get the ball through a series of obstacles, we win (non-Zero sum). For some, this will boil down to competition either with the system or with other players, cooperation, or collaboration.

You can summarise the three important distinctions between games and play as:

- Prelusory goals: Games have goals to achieve as set by an external source such as the game designer.
- Lusory means: Games have rules that define how you must achieve these prelusory goals.
- Constitutive rules: Games have rules that create challenges that must be completed to achieve goals. Rather than going from A to B in a straight line, you must overcome obstacles and solve puzzles going A to Z to E to B and back again!

Bringing It All Together

Put simply, the relationships between games, play and toys can be written like this;

- You play.
- You play a game.
- You play with a toy.
- You play a game with a toy.

Figure 1 is my attempt to summarise all of this as neatly as possible.

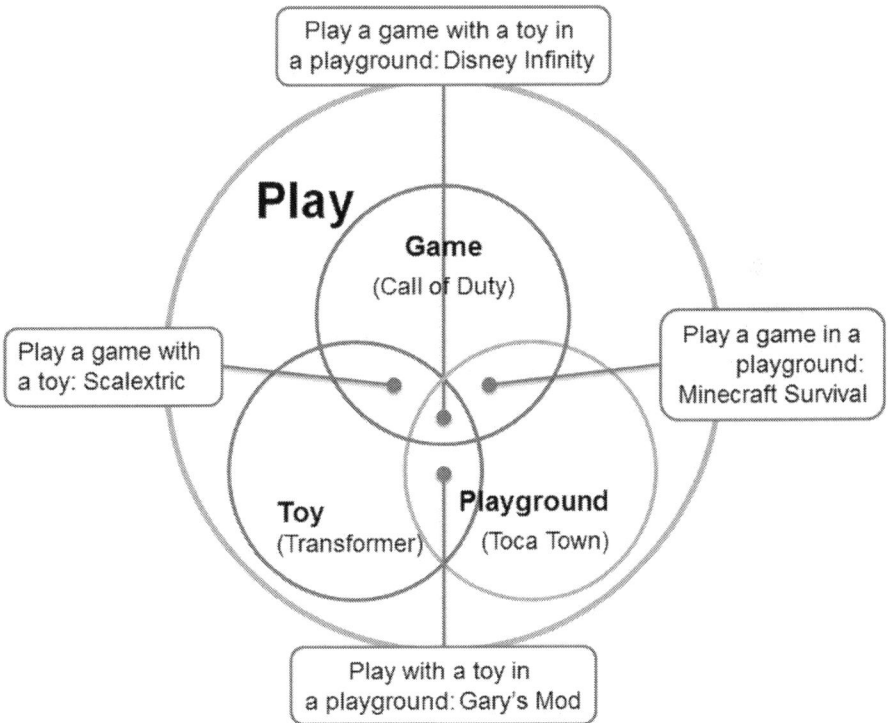

Figure 1 Play, Games and Toys

Play in Context

The concept of play is very important to me. I feel that it is one of the true keys to engagement in adults, but it often seems that adults often have no idea how to play. They have the intrinsic desire to play battered out of them by the "real" world. Unlike children, they often don't see the potential for play in the world around them. Some blame work for this – they often say that the opposite of play is work. However, I prefer to go with Dr Stuart Brown's (founder of the National Institute of Play) analysis in this case, that the opposite of play is actually depression [20].

Work is actually very similar to play and even more like games. The main difference is perception. We speak about lusory attitude a lot where play and games are concerned. As mentioned earlier, this is where you approach a non-play situation with a playful attitude. Just this change in mindset can change your perception of a situation. Therefore, with the right attitude, work can seem much more playful or gameful (note – these are not the same thing!!!)

Playfulness vs Gamefulness

First and foremost, Playfulness and Gamefulness both need a safe environment. Playfulness requires a great deal of freedom and a lack of explicit rules imposed by the system or environment. In contrast, Gamefulness is a little less freeform, there are explicit rules that are maintained by the system.

Play Sits Between Chaos and Control

Over the years I have concluded that play sits between chaos and control in the context of the world within which play is occurring. It is not totally without rules, but it is also not totally beholden to them.

However, as I dove deeper into thinking about where play sits in our understanding of the world and how we react to it. I realised that it is not quite as simple as chaos and control, it also had a lot to do with intent. Did we explicitly mean to do something or is it more implicit in nature? It occurred to me that play also sits between implicit and explicit desires and actions. We play at a conscious and subconscious level.

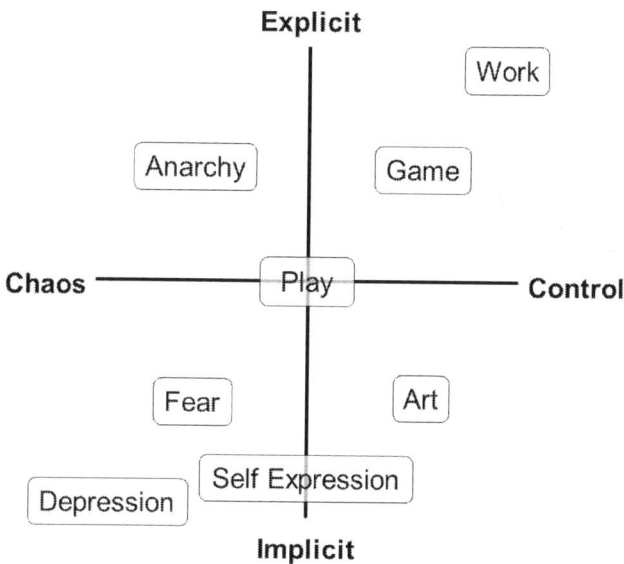

Figure 2 Play in Context

I mapped out a few other concepts to give this more context. For instance, I see anarchy as a deliberate act that leads to chaos. **Art** is implicit to the artist, that is it comes from the soul. However, the artist must have a level of control from the artist. They must get their ideas down in a way that fits their vision. That takes control.

Fear is an internal emotion that often comes from a lack of control – from chaos, not understanding what is happening around us. And we all know what fear leads to (puts on a *Yoda Voice*) *"Fear is the path to the dark side. Fear leads to anger. Anger leads to hate. Hate leads to suffering."* At the far end of this, we find **depression**, a complete loss of all control in every way.

Self-expression is also internal but sits between chaos and control. Think of an artist who covers themselves in paint and rolls around on a sheet of paper. Whilst they have an idea and have some level of control – there is a random, chaotic nature to it as well.

At the other end of the scale, we have **games**. They have a much more explicit control of the player's experience. The reason this is not at the far top right is because there the player still has some freedom in most, if not all, games. However, with **work**, this seems to be much less the case – especially in more "traditional" jobs. Explicit Control rules!

As you can finally see, **Play** sits somewhere in the middle of all of this. It is implicit, explicit, chaotic and controlled all at once. Hey, I didn't say it was simple!

So What?

This is all very philosophical, but there is a useful point to this. To get the best out of people you need to allow them a level of autonomy, but not so much that it descends into chaos, There also needs to be a level of control, but not so much that they are unable to make decisions for themselves. This balance helps to give them the freedom they need, within a framework that supports them.

Types of Rules in Play and Games

As mentioned, play is not devoid of rules. It is just that the rules seem less obvious to the observer. When talking about play, this perceived lack of rules is often emphasised as a big difference between games and play. Not everyone is quite as black and white on that, myself included. What play lacks is what I refer to as system rules. It is still beholden to other types of rules, what I am now calling inherent rules and meta-rules.

Inherent Rules

Inherent rules are those rules that affect play or toys in ways that are not controlled by outside influences; such as a player or a game designer. For instance, a ball has several inherent rules. It is affected by gravity, it has mass, volume, wind resistance etc. These things are all inherent to the ball. In a game like Minecraft, the inherent rules of the game would include how high you can build, how deep you can dig, what you must combine to make certain objects. The player plays within these inherent rules.

System Rules

System rules are rules that are added by the player or the designer that are there to create the game. If you are bouncing a ball seemingly aimlessly, this could be considered play. The inherent rules control the activity more than anything. How high the ball can bounce, for example? If you then decided that you must bounce the ball as high as you can and catch it with your left hand, you are adding system rules, you are creating a simple game. You are deliberately adding an obstruction to just bouncing the ball and catching it!

Meta-Rules

These are rules that go beyond what you would consider written or system-imposed rules. These are fluid rules that can change moment by moment. These are the rules that define how play unfolds. They are the unspoken rules that children manage to communicate to each other when they are playing. The situation is constantly changing, but they always seem to be able to adapt to the changes without fuss. Mrs Dawkin's tea party takes a sinister turn as Action Man invades and takes Teddy Ruckspin hostage. These are rules about rules, rules beyond rules, unspoken rules, unwritten rules and quite frankly – unfathomable rules to those not involved directly in the play!

Toys/Play/Games

I don't consider just games and play on their own, I always include toys. Toys can be an essential part of games and play. Toys are just objects.

They have inherent rules, as I said earlier, but really, they must have other rules associated with them to be included in play and games. A ball does not play with itself and is certainly not a game without some kind of system rules. On their own, they just have inherent rules.

Play, as discussed has inherent rules and these meta-rules. Games have system rules as well as inherent rules. A toy can exist without play or games, play can exist without toys or games. Games, however, must have play to exist.

In diagrammatic form (as is my way) this looks a bit like the following

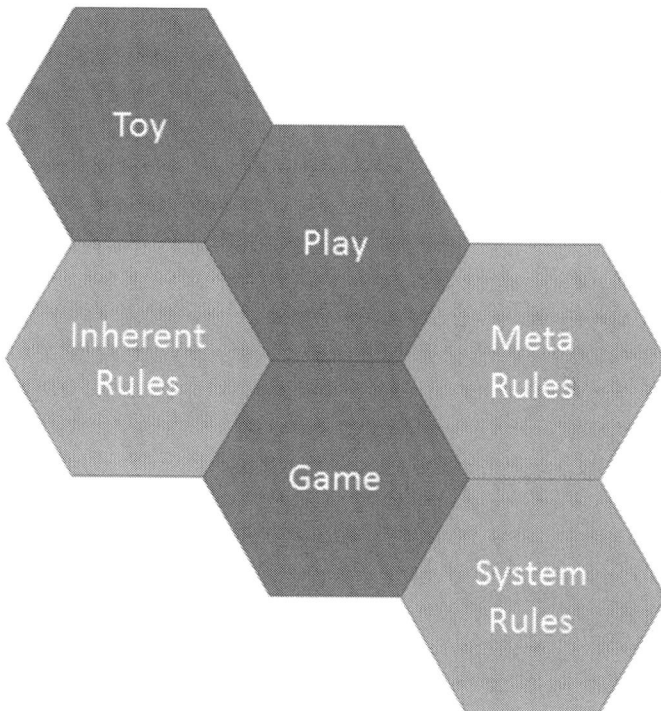

Figure 3 Play, Toys and Games

Inherent rules affect games, play and toys. Meta-rules affect play, and in turn games (you can't have a game without play!). Finally, system rules that only affect games.

The Meta-Rules of Play

Having introduced the concept of Meta-Rules, it seems sensible to expand on them a little. As a reminder, these were the non-system or inherent rules that guide how people play.

I have broken them down into four categories; social, contextual, communication and personal.

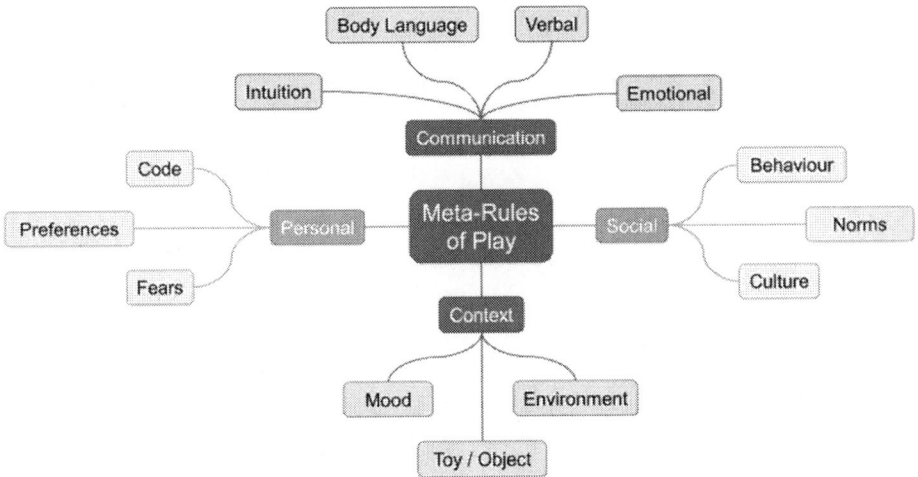

Figure 4 The Meta Rules of Play

Communication

Communication and empathy play an enormous part in collaborative play. I have identified four types that help to control play.

- **Verbal**
  - The most obvious form of communication – yelling instructions or updates!
- **Intuition**
  - Sensing how others are reacting to you and those around them, that feeling that you know something has changed based on subtle hints from others.
- **Body Language**
  - Almost as unsubtle as verbal communication, you can tell what other people playing are feeling with how they appear. Crossed arms, looking unhappy, looking to the left to indicate where you should go next etc.
- **Emotional**
  - A layer on top of other types of communication and similar in style to intuition, emotional communication is understanding the emotional subtext of other types of communication. A player may communicate in a happy way, but there could be other underlying emotions.

Social

Social meta-rules are more about what society expects. When playing, there are some things that others don't expect – based on social rules.

Whilst I have broken these down into three headings, they are all linked. There is an expected behaviour based on culture and the norms for that culture.

For instance, if you are play acting mummy's and daddy's, it would be very unexpected by most cultural norms and standards for one player to jump up and start pretending to shoot all the others!

Context

Play is contextual, it can change depending on where people are, what they are playing with and how they feel.

- **Environment**
  - o What are the surroundings whilst playing? How does that affect what can and can't be done? It's the difference between playing catch in a field and catch on a cliff edge!
- **Mood**
  - o The mood of the people playing can change rapidly, this can then change the emphasis of play and how others react to play. If you are playing alone with dolls and are happy, you may be making up stories of going to the beach. If you are sad or have been traumatised, your play acting may take a darker turn.
- **Toy / Object**
  - o If you are playing with a toy of some sort, that can drastically change what you are playing. It may be fun to bounce a ball off a wall, but less so if you are then handed a wooden block instead!

Personal

Everyone is different and what they find enjoyable or fun is also very different. Each person has their own preferences, personal code (i.e. moral code or code of conduct) and of course fears.

- **Code**
    - o This is what a player is prepared to do based on their own moral judgement. Some kids may not want to be involved in certain types of play, just as adults may not! This will guide how they react during play and the ever-changing meta-rules!
- **Preferences**
    - o As I say, not everyone is the same. Some may like to play with a ball, others would prefer to act out plays with dolls.
- **Fears**
    - o Fear is a great motivator. That example of playing catch on a cliff. I would not do it, but some might!

A lot of things in life are very game-like in nature, especially work. There are strict rules about how tasks must be completed. Completion of tasks and compliance with rules is rewarded (you get paid), breaking these rules leads to negative consequences (reprimands, warnings, getting fired).

What we don't see very often is the more play-like side of games being included in real-world tasks such as work. The lack of structure, the freedom to experiment and more importantly, to fail, are all missing.

Very often what we are doing in gamification is trying to inject some more play into these types of system. Elements that are fun just because they are fun, simulated environments to allow failure and learning in safety, more freedom to experiment and innovate etc. Of course, on top of that, we are adding elements that make things feel a bit more like a game. Adding new purpose, rapid feedback, increased interactivity, concentrating on Flow (explained later) and more.

As an adult, with children of my own, it is interesting to see how adults deal with situations that children find simple. I have seen grown men reduced to arguments in projects because no one set certain rules. For some reason, their mature ways of thinking have evolved to preclude imagination totally. If they are not told exactly what to do, they just can't cope and think their way out of a situation they have not been programmed to deal with.

On the flip side, my eldest daughter in the absence of rules just tries stuff. If it doesn't work, she tries something else. She learns as she goes, knowing that each failure just gives her one less thing to try next time. Sure, it can lead to frustration and tears, but that doesn't stop her trying again.

Sometimes we need rules and fixed experiences, sometimes we just need to be allowed to try things for ourselves – exercise our imaginations.

Remind adults how to play, let them explore and give them a level of freedom and autonomy. I am not suggesting you give them an open sandbox at work and a $6,000,000 budget to blow but give them a chance to experiment and get things wrong.

Let them play!

What Are Game Mechanics?

When I do play games, I need to understand the rules. It turns out that games folk call these mechanics. Either way, knowing how a game works gives me a great chance of winning. Just wait Andrzej, just wait...

Game mechanics are often spoken about in gamification, but their meaning is often lost, misunderstood or misapplied. I want to take a slightly academic look at what they really are and their relationship with gamification.

What Are Game Mechanics?

To understand why this might be let's first look at what game mechanics are. The following are quotes taken from various well-known game design books and papers.

"Core Mechanics represent the essential moment-to-moment activity of players. During a game, core mechanics create patterns of repeated behaviour, the experiential building blocks of play." Katie Salen and Eric Zimmerman: *Rules of Play* [19]

"Mechanics are the various actions, behaviours and control mechanisms afforded to the player within a game context. The mechanics support overall gameplay dynamics" Robin Hunicke, Marc LeBlanc & Robert Zubek: *MDA Framework* [21]

"These are the procedures and rules of your game. Mechanics describe the goal of your game, how players can and cannot try to achieve it, and what happens when they try." Jesse Schell: *The Art of Game Design, A Book of Lenses* [18]

For our purposes, we can distil the definition down to:

> "A distinct set of rules that dictate the outcome of interactions within the system. They have an input, a process and an output."

Further to this, we can also state that dynamics are:

> *"The user's response to collections of these mechanics"*

For example, consider *Space Invaders*.

- **Input**: User hits fire
- **Process/rules**: Bullet speed, bullet vector, position of enemy
- **Output**: Miss; nothing. Hit; explosion, score increase.

If we apply the same logic to a simple gamification concept often called a mechanic, Epic Meaning, we can see that there is an issue.

Epic Meaning is something I use in gamification all the time, creating a sense that what you are asking of the user has a purpose or meaning greater than just their current activity.

- **Input**: Well, it does not really have one. A person is in the system
- **Process/rules:** creating an atmosphere or narrative around meaning. This would break down into many different elements in the system.
- **Output:** The user feels a sense of purpose and greater meaning

It does not really fit.

The reality is that you cannot break something like Epic Meaning down like this, so it is not a mechanic. It is the outcome of many different mechanics and interactions within a well-designed system. Look at our *Space Invaders* example a little more closely and see what else is going on.

- "User hits fire". This requires an interface initially, that takes the user's inputs and interprets them. This then triggers the creation of a bullet graphic on-screen.

- "Bullet speed, bullet vector, the position of the enemy". The programmed rules of the game dictate how fast the bullet will travel; the position of the player will determine the exact direction it will take. More programmed rules will tell the game where the enemies are and if the bullet has hit them.

- "Miss, nothing. Hit: explosion, score increase". If the bullet misses, obviously nothing happens. If it hits an enemy (which will have several rules defining the hit area), there will be some sort of visual feedback. If the enemy only takes one hit to kill, you get an explosion. If it takes more, you will get some sort of other feedback showing you were successful but have more to do. You will also get more feedback showing you an increase in score. If it is the last enemy, you may also move on to the next level (progression).

Is there something like this in gamification? Yes, there are mechanics, but they are hidden deep in the system. As a gamification designer, you are often considering the dynamics and the aesthetics or emotions of the user for whom you are designing, less than the mechanics.

A very simple example, where we want to increase the number of Likes content on a brand's Facebook page gets. We will use the old classic: points, badges and leaderboards.

Clicking the "Like" button gives you points. Points are used as the basis for getting badges and position within a Leaderboard.

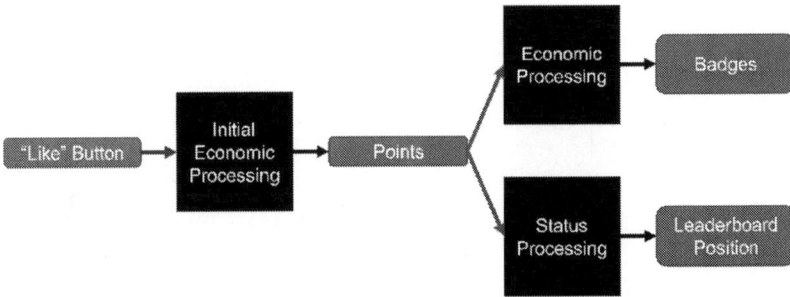

Figure 5 Simple Gamification Mechanics

There are several mechanics involved here.

Clicking the button to receive a reward is a mechanic. Changing the balance of the mechanic would then change how many points are given to the user for a click.

These points are then processed through two secondary mechanics. The first awards badges/trophies based on how many points the user now has. The second takes the points and works out where the user now sits on a leaderboard, giving them some level of status.

Progress bars, images of badges and leaderboards are just visual aids to monitor feedback, not game mechanics.

Considering Gamification

A popular framework within game design is the MDA framework, mentioned earlier. MDA stands for Mechanics, Dynamics and Aesthetics. Whilst designed specifically for games, the MDA framework can still be of use in gamification. Below is a slight expansion that I have found helpful, starting at the system and ending at the user.

- **Mechanics**: A set of rules that define what can be done in the system. These are defined by the designer.
- **Schedules**: Rules that define how and when certain events happen in the system, such as how many points lead to the next level, when badges are given, needing to have X & Y to get Z etc.
- **Dynamics**: How the mechanics and the user act together in real-time. Mostly out of the designer's control and can lead to unexpected/emergent outcomes.
- **Feedback**: Representation of the results from actions taken in the system. Points, badges, progress bars, messages.
- **Tokens**: Virtual items. Rewards, collectables and even points are all tokens.
- **Interactions**: Points of contact between the user and the system, such as a mouse click.
- **Aesthetics**: The emotional response of the user to the system. Joy, fear, frustration etc.

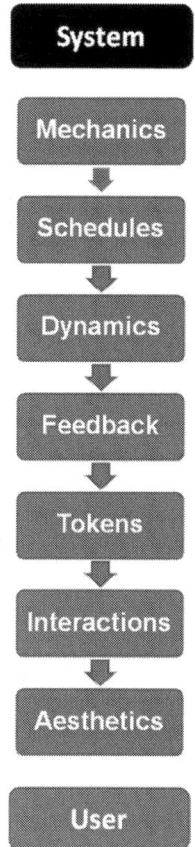

System

Mechanics

Schedules

Dynamics

Feedback

Tokens

Interactions

Aesthetics

User

Taking a common gamification example, how could these be used to describe a hashtag-based competition, tweeting a hashtag to the most people?

- **Mechanics**: Calculation of user tweet and retweet totals.
- **Schedules**: After 10 retweets of the hashtag, the user gets a badge. Final win condition.
- **Dynamics**: Some users may spam their networks if there are no explicit rules preventing them, i.e. the "game" allows it.
- **Feedback**: Users are sent an email to thank them. They are also given points, badges and a position on a leaderboard.
- **Tokens**: The user is given redeemable points.
- **Interactions**: The user creates a tweet with the correct hashtag and then sends it.
- **Aesthetics**: Some users will enjoy being on the leaderboard. Others may be frustrated by how other users decide to play and how *fair* the system seems.

Obviously, there is a lot more going in, but you can see the basics there and why it is so hard to talk about real mechanics in gamification. I have not even spoken about the fact we need to consider motivation of the user to do something. Many of the things that are spoken about as mechanics are really motivations or drives!

What is Fun?

What you find fun, I may not – are you into swinging
from the trees and eating bananas with your feet?

Fun

According to the dictionary, fun is *"Enjoyment, amusement, or light-hearted pleasure"* [22]. To you or me though, fun can have lots of meanings. It could be watching your children play in the garden, reading a book, playing games or just walking in the park. Fun is completely subjective and is different for us all.

The reason fun is sitting here after game mechanics is because of its relationship to the MDA framework. Marc LeBlanc talks about Eight Kinds of Fun [23] and their relation to aesthetics or the emotional response to the interaction of the player with the game mechanics.

Eight Kinds of Fun

Sensation Game as sense-pleasure	**Fellowship** Game as social framework
Fantasy Game as make-believe	**Discovery** Game as uncharted territory
Narrative Game as an unfolding story	**Expression** Game as soapbox
Challenge Game as an obstacle course	**Submission** Game as mindless pastime

Nicole Lazzaro has one of my favourite views on fun – the 4 Keys 2 Fun. More than just labels, this describes how users experience fun and how to design games to enhance that.

Nicole Lazzaro's 4 Keys 2 Fun

People Fun (Friendship)	Easy Fun (Novelty)
Amusement from competition and cooperation	Curiosity from exploration, role play, and creativity
Hard Fun (Challenge)	**Serious Fun (Meaning)**
Fiero, the epic win, from achieving a difficult goal	Excitement from changing the player and their world

Of course, I have my own version of what fun is and means. A small survey I conducted highlighted 21 experiences that people described as fun, split into the five groups of fun.

Achievement Fun

Curiosity	Learning
Wanting to know what is in the box, what happens next, what is around the corner.	Gaining knowledge, learning new skills - mastery.
Problem Solving	**Challenge**
Puzzles, use of problem-solving (specifically) to overcome challenges.	Overcoming obstacles. Attaining a sense of achievement.

Free Spirited Fun

Exploration	Discovery
Deliberately looking around and testing the boundaries.	Finding new or interesting things, deliberately or not.
Surprise The joy of the unexpected.	**Creativity** Building, inventing, creating new stuff like music or art.

Social Fun

Family	Collaboration
Joy from your relatives. Love.	Working with others on a common goal.
Fellowship Relatedness. Being with others.	**Competition** You vs. the world.
Altruism Selfless acts towards others, sense of greater purpose.	

Facilitated, Personal Fun

Narrative	**Progression**
Stories and plot lines.	The feeling that you are moving towards a goal.
Fantasy	**Immersion**
Make believe, such as worlds created by books, film or imagination.	Believing in a fantasy world totally and losing yourself to it.

Un-Facilitated, Personal Fun

Humour	**Sensation**
Different for everyone, but jokes, funny stories and situations.	Joy in physical sensation. Smell, activity, sport, touch etc.
Schadenfreude	**Flow**
Pleasure in the suffering of others.	As described by Mihaly Csikszentmihalyi, losing your sense of self in an activity.

As you can see, you can look at fun in many ways. In my view, gamification is not about making things more fun. Fun can certainly be part of a solution, but that is not its key purpose.

That said, understanding that what you find fun others may find embarrassing or annoying, is key to you designing experiences that more people are likely to engage with.

What is Game Thinking?

Like many, my Master used to use gamification as an umbrella term for all game-based solutions. Then, thinking he was clever, he came up with Game Thinking as an alternative catch-all.

Gamification is often used as a catch-all for games-based solutions. In theory, this is not a problem, but it can confuse people as to what gamification is. That is why Game Thinking is such an important concept in how I personally view gamification and other game-based solutions. I define Game Thinking in the following way;

"The use of games and game-like approaches to solve problems and create better experiences."

Those problems could be *"how do we engage a new audience"* or *"how do we help people get to the next stage of this learning"*. Game Thinking contains four main categories: Gamification, Game Inspired/Playful Design, Serious Games and Games.

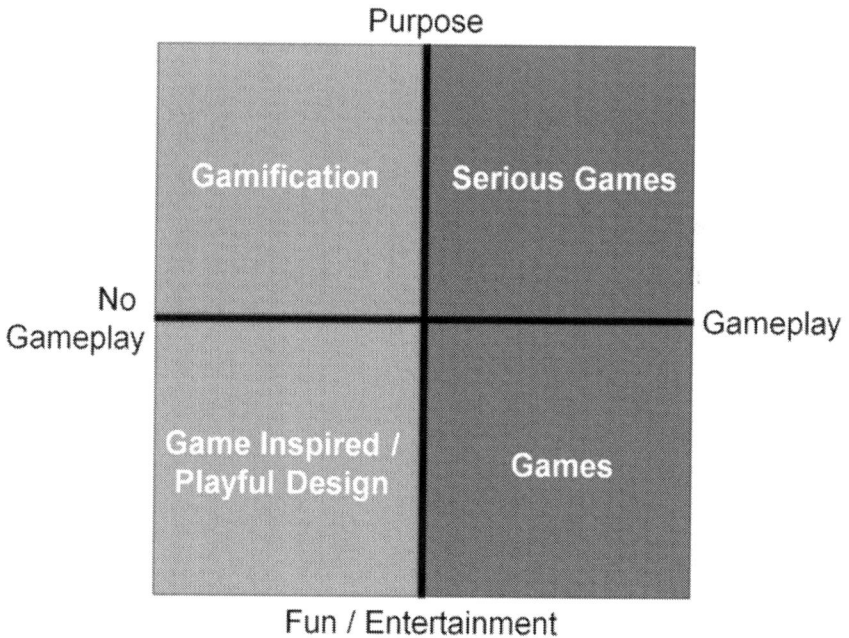

Figure 6 Game Thinking by Intent

The categorisations consider the original design intent of the products, whether it was designed to be just for entertainment or for a purpose. Also, the inclusion of gameplay is considered.

For instance, in Figure 6, Serious Games contain gameplay, the "thing" that really makes a game, where pure gamification does not. However, both are created for a primary purpose other than fun or entertainment.

For the sake of clarity, a fifth category can be added to game-based solutions, simulations.

Each of these five segments can then be further broken down.

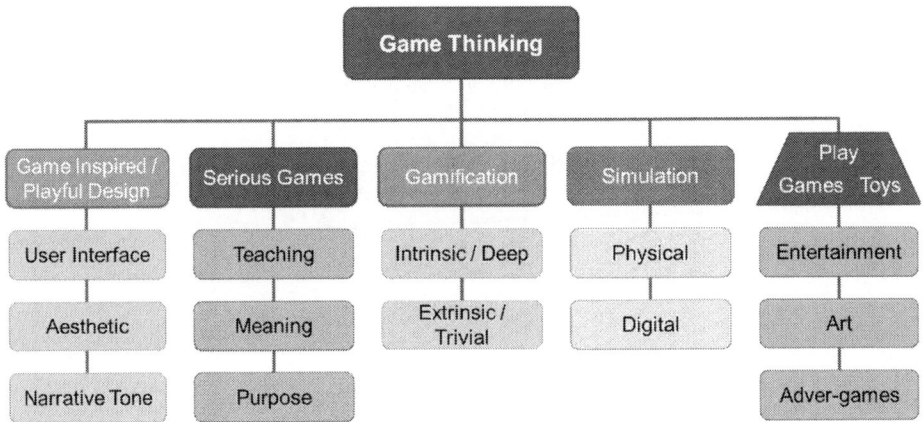

Figure 7 Game Thinking

Gamification and Game Thinking in Practice

Now that you understand what my Master thinks game thinking is, how about I show you some examples of it in action. He sure as hell won't bother!

Serious Games

This group includes full games that have been created for reasons other than pure entertainment. Here I split them into four basic types.

Teaching Games

This is a type of game designed to teach the player something, for example, arithmetic, coding, or zoology, by playing a real game. Unlike a simulation, it does not have to be representative of the real world. For example, *Phantomation* is a game that teaches the player how to use the animation software *Play Sketch*. Rather than just showing you the tools or simulating them in a dry way, it has you solving various puzzles that need deeper and deeper understanding of the tool as the game progresses. It plays well as a game in its own right.

Figure 8 Phantomation

Game Inspired/Playful Design

This is where no actual elements from games are used, just ideas. For example, user interfaces that mimic those from games, design or artwork that is inspired by games or the way language is used. It can also be the inclusion of "playful" elements. These do not affect the workings of the system but are there just for some fun. You can see a nice example of this on the *Toca Boca* website.

On their website, they have a novel way to scroll from the bottom of the page back to the top. Rather than the more common arrow to click, there is a balloon. When you click this, it floats from the bottom of the page back to the top, dragging the screen with it. All these concepts have links to games but lack anything that you would consider part of the inner workings of a game (mechanics, dynamics, tokens, etc.)

I look a little more deeply at play and playfulness elsewhere in the book.

Figure 9 www.tocaboca.com

Meaningful Game/Games for Good

This is a group of games that attempts to get across a meaningful message and promote change with that message. An example of this would be *Darfur is Dying*. This was the result of a competition run by the Reebok Human Rights Foundation and the International Crisis Group [24]. The winning game came from five students from the University of Southern California that placed you in the shoes of a displaced Darfurian refugee. It aimed to show the hardships faced by the millions of people displaced by the crisis in Sudan.

Rather than trying to teach you a tool or a method of doing something, this type of game is trying to inform you about ideas that may never have crossed your mind in a way that is engaging and meaningful.

Figure 10 Darfur is Dying

Purposeful Game

The idea of a purposeful game is that playing it has some sort of real-world outcome. Three examples of this come to mind: *FoldIt, Tilt World* and *Genes in* Space from Cancer Research UK. *FoldIt* is a popular game often cited by gamification advocates. Developed by the University of Washington, *FoldIt* is a puzzle game that sets the player the task of predicting the structure of proteins by folding them.

Understanding how proteins fold can help lead to the development of cures for all sorts of diseases, including HIV and cancer. Humans are good at solving puzzles; so good that in just ten days, gamers had solved one enzymatic structure, potentially a key to curing AIDS, that scientists had been trying to unravel for more than a decade via more traditional methods [25].

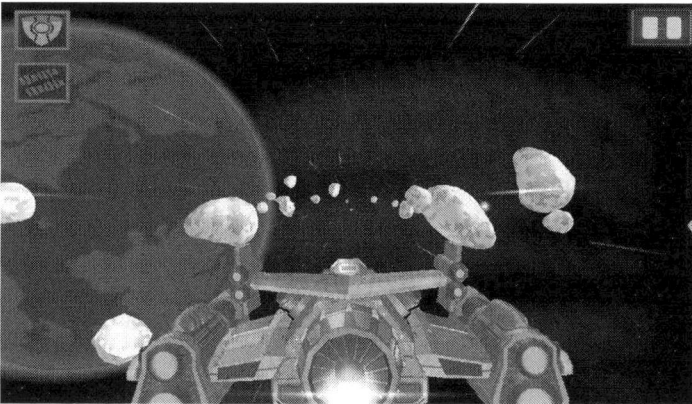

Figure 11 Genes in Space

Tilt World, by Nicole Lazzaro, is a mobile game that puts you in the body of the last tadpole – Flip.

You must eat carbon from the air in an attempt to restore the sunshine to Flip's home. Although this may seem like a meaningful game, in that it is trying to promote a message about ecology, the unique thing about *Tilt World* is that playing it leads to the planting of actual trees in Madagascar [26]. As a final example, *Genes in Space* is a space shooter game that uses gameplay to map genomes to help the fight against cancer in the real world! [27]

A Quick Summary

- **Teaching Game:** Teaches using real games and gameplay.
- **Meaningful Game:** Uses gameplay to promote a meaningful message to the player.
- **Purposeful Game:** Uses games to create direct real-world outcomes.

Gamification

As explained earlier, gamification is about taking ideas and elements from games and using them in non-game contexts. I split this into two basic types. Intrinsic deep and Extrinsic trivial. This is very similar to Karl Kapp's two types of gamification [28], where he talks about structural and content gamification.

Trivial gamification is what most people are used to, where game elements are bolted on to a system. You will often see points, badges, progress bars, and the like.

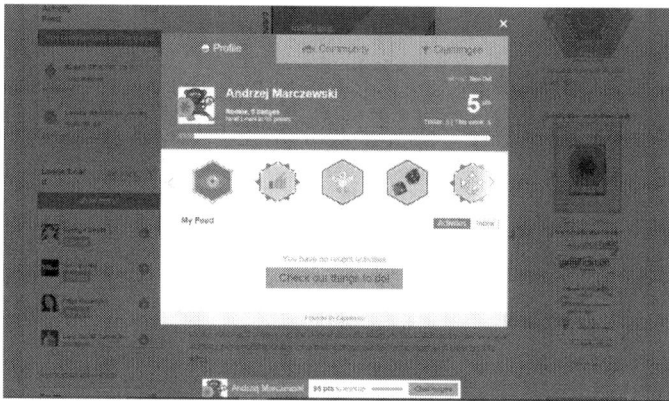

Figure 12 Gamified UK with Trivial Layer Gamification

Figure 12 shows my own website, with a simple Trivial Layer implementation of gamification. It has points, badges, leaderboards and more.

Intrinsic deep gamification is more about using motivation and behavioural design to engage users.

A good example of this can be seen in question and answer sites such as *Quora* or *Stack Exchange*, where points and the like are used to reinforce particular behaviours but do not form the basis for people contributing.

Simulation

A simulation is a virtual representation of something from the real world, such as a flight simulator. Often this can be hard to distinguish from a game or a serious game, as they look very game like. The difference is that a simulation does not usually need gameplay elements in order to function and fulfil its designed intent. It exists to allow users to practice an activity in a safe environment.

Simulations are not a new phenomenon either, with military simulations in one form or another used since the start of organised warfare. The birth of modern wargames and simulations has been credited to Herr von Reisswitz, Prussian War Counsellor and his war game *Kriegsspiel* in 1812 [29]. This was a military game/simulation that each regiment was encouraged to play on a regular basis to test out strategies and tactics without having to risk troops.

Simulations can take many forms; physical such as board games or role-playing, digital like computer-based flight simulations or business simulations or blended where you have a bit of both as in augmented reality.

Games/Play/Toys

Games, play and toys are explained in more detail in the next chapter, however, it is useful to see a short summary of them here.

- Play is free form and has no extrinsically imposed goals. It is undertaken for fun or joy.
- Games add defined goals and rules to play, like challenges.
- Toys are objects that can be used in play or games.

Concentrating on games, I categorise them into three basic types.

Entertainment

Entertainment is what most people would associate with games. *Call of Duty, Civilization* or *World of Warcraft* for example. They are designed with the intention of entertaining people in some way, with no deliberate higher purpose.

Art

Art is subjective. I would consider a game such as *Proteus* more art than game where some would not. *Proteus* is a game with little to no gameplay but creates a beautiful and thoughtful experience. It is entertainment but done in a way that evokes different kinds of emotions to those of standard games.

Adver-Games

These are proper games created to advertise something. The game is a real game, but at some stage, it is being used to try to sell you something. An example I enjoyed playing, was *Elfridges*, an old-school platformer in the style of *Super Mario*, designed to raise awareness of Selfridges and its various locations [30].

The Game Thinking Spectrum

With all of that said and highlighting all the differences between various game-based solutions, a good gamification practitioner will look at the problem they are given and decide what the best solution is for their client based on their needs, not on the semantics surrounding the difference between gamification and serious games. It is all a spectrum that flows and can be mixed and matched as needed.

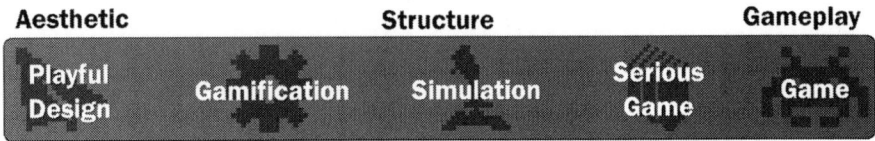

Aesthetic		Structure		Gameplay
Playful Design	Gamification	Simulation	Serious Game	Game

Figure 13 The Game Thinking Spectrum

Aesthetic: At this end of the spectrum, the solutions share the look and at times the feel of games, they are more "game-like" than they are game.

Structure: Around the mid-point, the solution will not only have the look of a game, they will also share structural comparisons. Challenges, narratives, scoring systems, RPG elements, feedback, progress etc.

Gameplay: As we move to the gameplay end of the spectrum, the solutions are more game than game-like. They have true gameplay and all the trappings one would expect with a true game, whether it is for more serious purposes or for pure entertainment.

Ethical Considerations of Gamification

How ethical is it to keep and train a monkey? Well, if that sort of question interests, then this chapter is for you. It discusses the ethics of gamification and offers some ways to think about them.

Gamification, the use of game elements in non-game contexts, has had its fair share of critics over the years. People have labelled it everything from shamification to exploitationware, fearing its use as nothing more than manipulation or exploitation. This has led people to question its ethical and moral implications.

Gamification is often viewed through a near dystopian lens. From Jesse Schell's 2010 DICE talk on the invasion of games [31] to Ernest Cline's *Ready Player One* and to Charlie Brooker's *Black Mirror*, it seems that the only outcome for a world where gamification is prevalent is a negative one.

This presents several questions when we are considering designing gamification-based solutions. First, what are ethics and how do we evaluate solutions against them? The next crucial question is what are the responsibilities of the designer? Should they be held accountable for the way people choose to use their system or does their responsibility start and end with the design?

This has been discussed in academic literature a few times; here I wish to look at the ethics of gamification from a layman's perspective.

Defining Ethics

The use of the correct terminology is important to understanding one's perspective in an argument for or against something. With that in mind, it is of use to clearly define what is meant by *ethics*.

As noted by ethics researchers Richard Paul and Linder Elder, many confuse ethics with social, religious or political norms rather than treating ethics as a standalone set of principles. Instead, Paul and Elder consider ethics as *"[a] set of concepts and principles that guide us in determining what behaviour helps or harms sentient creatures"* [32].

At a basic level, ethics are external rules or guidelines where morals are more personal and inherent to an individual. It may be *ethically* acceptable to consume meat, but to a vegetarian, it may be *morally* unacceptable. For the purpose of this discussion and with relation to the design of gamification and gamified systems, ethics will be defined as *"a set of principles to facilitate the design of solutions that, on balance, promote desirable outcomes for the users."*

The emphasis here is on the intention of the gamification designer to create systems that help rather than bring harm to others, though defining harm is potentially subjective. When you build things, you can often become so attached to them that you become blind to potential criticism or dangers. Therefore, it is useful to have frameworks and ethical guidelines, preventing the potential inherent dangers of personal morals, or lack thereof, over-ruling ethics.

Ethics Framework

To discuss the ethics of a system, we need to have a framework to decide what constitutes help and harm to others. Based on our definition of ethics, I have proposed the following simple framework for discussion.

- Does the system offer a choice?
- What is the intention of the designer?
- What are the potential positive and negative outcomes of being in the system?
- Are the beneficial outcomes weighted towards the needs or desires of the user or the designer?

Discussion by Example

A social credit system has been proposed in China, to be rolled out and mandatory by 2020, called Sesame Credit. The premise of Sesame Credit is to give every citizen of China a score, based on how "good" a citizen they are. This score is based on many factors, including what the user purchases through Alibaba, the country's largest online retailer. Technology director of Sesame, Li Yingyun, in an interview with the Chinese magazine *Caixin* said, *"Someone who plays video games for 10 hours a day, for example, would be considered an idle person, and someone who frequently buys diapers would be considered as probably a parent, who on balance is more likely to have a sense of responsibility"* [33].

This scenario was extrapolated out in a video from Extra Credit titled *Propaganda Games: Sesame Credit,* where this social credit score could be based on what people do on social media, what they purchase and potentially more crucially, who they are friends with.

The answer to the first questions here is twofold. Initially, Sesame Credit will be voluntary. However, by 2020, it would be mandatory. Initially participants would have free will and be able to choose to join or not, but that choice will eventually be taken away. It could also be argued that making it voluntary initially will create a FOMO (fear of missing out) effect, with early adopters imposing social pressure on those who have not already joined.

The intention of the system is more complex to analyse. On the surface, this is like any other credit score, informative to the owner of the score. Knowing their score and what can improve it is of benefit to the user, especially if higher scores could potentially lead to preferential treatment in the future. With this in mind, it could be argued that the intention of the system and indeed the potential outcomes for the user are both positive and good. Going back to our definition, on balance the outcomes are desirable.

However, when you consider how the system could be used to rate your relationships and potentially monitor all your online life, things start to twist away from benefiting the user and become much more focused on benefiting the designer. Whilst participation in the system may not directly harm the user, the potential outcomes could have a net negative effect on them. For instance, a low social score could lead to the loss of friends and the loss of services.

This does not consider the cultural differences in China compared to other countries and it is worth noting that for some, the idea of a social credit system is positive. But the potential outcomes for the user are less than ideal and arguably the intention of the design is not to benefit the users but to benefit the state. Therefore, it fails our definition of being ethical.

The second example for discussion is the game Pokémon Go. Whilst this is not a gamified system, it does share traits with gamification and opens interesting questions about the intention of the design.

Pokémon Go is a mixed reality game that sees players using their mobile devices exploring the real world to capture virtual Pokémon. By physically moving to different locations, players can find Pokémon and attempt to capture them.

However, the game has not been without controversy. Indeed, there were several major issues early on, including deaths related to playing the game. These incidents occurred when players were so desperate to capture Pokémon that they behaved in very unsafe ways; in one fatal case, a player broke into a person's house. This led to online discussions and articles condemning the designers for not having more forethought about the unintended consequences of playing Pokémon Go. The main argument raised was: should the designers take responsibility for the actions of the players, if the players put themselves in harm's way to play the game?

To consider the ethics of the game, we need to go back to our definition and framework. First, we must ask the question, does the game offer players a choice.

The answer is simple, yes. They do not *have* to download the game and play. Again, as with the social credit example, there is a fear of missing out and potential social pressure applied by early adopters. However, there is no danger of the game ever being made mandatory by the state!

Next, what was the intention of the designer when creating the game? In this instance, the answer is clear, to give joy to the players. They wanted to create a game that would get people physically involved in a new type of game. Of course, they also wanted to make money. This is not a negative point—it is the right of anyone creating new products to want to make a profit from them.

When considering the benefits and negative outcomes of being in the game, we can't ignore the fact that serious harm has befallen certain players. However, the majority have found the game to be enjoyable and have faced no negative effects of playing. So, on balance, the positive outcomes of being in the game far outweigh the potential negatives. This also is true of the benefits to the player vs that of the designer. The game was made to give joy to players and on balance, it seems that this is what it has done. The designers have made money, but not to the detriment of the player's enjoyment.

From an ethical standpoint, Pokémon Go does not seem to break our rules. The game was designed with good intent and players, on balance, benefit in the way they desire. However, there is a moral concern here. Whilst the negative events that transpired were unintended, they still happened. So, whilst there is no ethical issue (based on our definition), the designers did face a moral quandary.

To help limit the danger people faced playing the game, they created a series of messages that reminded the player not to do dangerous things whilst playing, such as not looking where they are going. Early in the game's life, there was also the question of where Pokestops and gyms where placed. For instance, was it acceptable to have a children's nursery marked on the map as a Pokestop as it could draw large numbers of people to the spot, not something that is desirable? Again, the developers took action, releasing tools to allow people to request the removal of Pokestops and gyms [34].

Pokémon Go represents an interesting crossroads in the argument around the ethics of designing systems. Whilst it did nothing deliberately wrong, it certainly had many unintended issues that could be considered the lack of forethought on the designer's part. Whether or not it is right to hold them responsible for this is a question of morality rather than ethics.

It is obvious that there are ethical concerns when it comes to the use of gamification. Whilst defining the term is of use, it helps to have a more expansive code of ethics for designers to consider when creating gamified solutions. There have been several created, notably by Zichermann and myself, although some feel that they do not always go as far as needed focussing more on the enterprise rather than the individual. However, the key elements that come out are a need for transparency and honesty with the user about the intentions of the system and not creating systems that deliberately trick users into behaviours that could cause them harm.

This is the main salient point about ethics and gamification. Gamification becomes unethical when the designer uses the psychology of players to manipulate them to do things that are not in their best interest. The use of random rewards to create addictive, gambling-like experiences that eventually lead certain users to be unable to exercise free will. Obfuscated systems that encourage users to divulge information about themselves for reasons that are not obviously stated initially. Systems that deliberately exploit those who are more vulnerable in society such as the sick or the very young.

It is very important to keep in mind that all these instances and indeed all instances of ethical concerns with gamification are not the fault of gamification as a concept, but rather the designer. Like a hammer, gamification is a tool. A hammer can be used to create beautiful works of art and to build houses when used by craftsmen who understand its uses and its limitations. However, a hammer can also be used to break objects and cause great damage when used by those with less creative intentions. This does not make the hammer ethical or unethical, it is just a tool. The ethics must be associated with the intentions of the person holding the hammer.

The same is true of gamification. The onus must be on the designer to use the techniques available to them in gamification in an ethical manner.

Originally Published in *XRDS: Crossroads, The ACM Magazine for Students Volume 24*

Issue 1, Fall 2017 Pages 56-59 doi: 10.1145/3123756 35

THE SCIENCE OF GAMIFICATION

What Motivates Us?

There are many levels of motivation, from survival to rewards. I have my own motivations and they may well be different to yours... they are certainly different to my Master's as he will soon discover.

Understanding what motivates people is a key concept in your gamification designs if you want them to succeed.

A lot of talk in gamification revolves around the relative values of extrinsic motivation, such as rewards and intrinsic motivation. It often seems like a conversation about good and evil! The truth is that both have their place, you just must tweak the balance and application of them.

There are many theories out there about what motivates us and how. For the purposes of gamification, I break these down into three distinct layers. These layers can help us to understand how and why certain types of gamification may or may not work.

Three Layers of Motivation

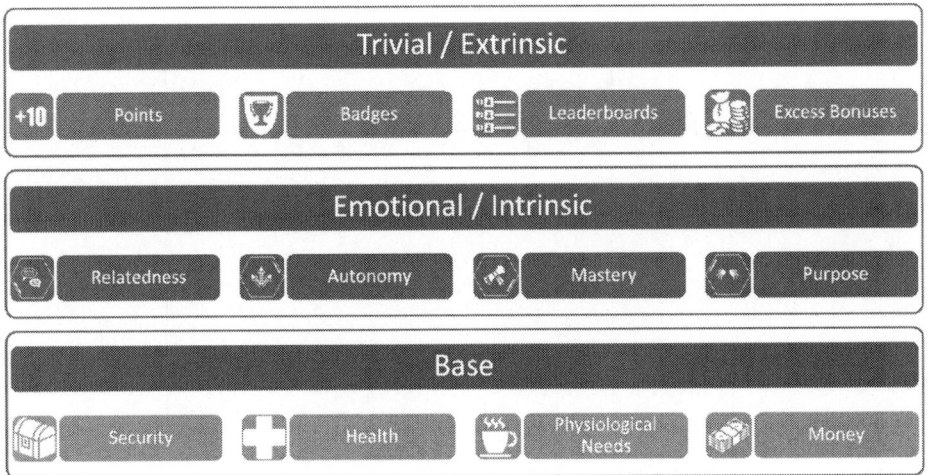

Figure 14 The Three Layers of Motivation

Base

It is hard to speak about motivation without mentioning Maslow's *Hierarchy of Needs* [36] as this is one of the best known of the models that describe human needs and motivations. Outlined in 1943, Maslow describes five levels of human needs: physiological, safety, belonging, esteem and self-actualisation. Although it has been criticised [37], it is a useful starting point for use when we consider why people behave in the way they do and how we can use that knowledge to create better experiences for them.

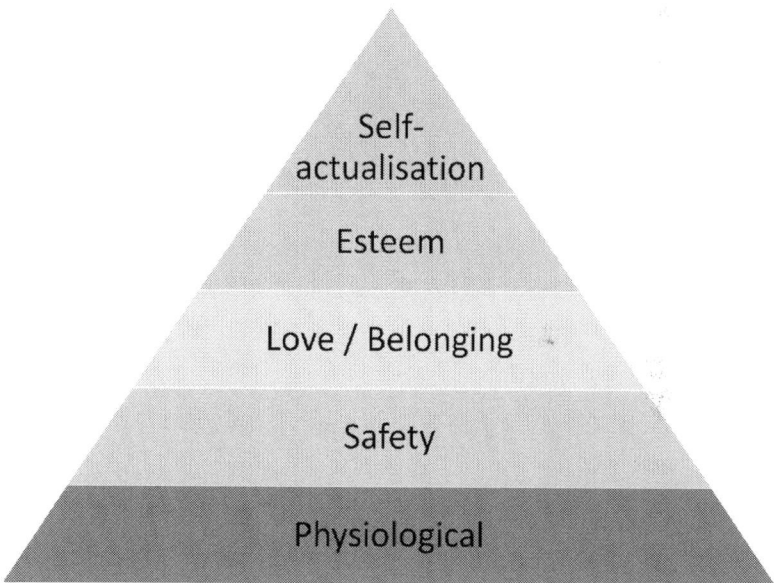

Figure 15 Maslow's Hierarchy of Needs

Physiological needs include air, water, sleep and procreation. Safety is more about securing yourself and your family. Belonging relates to our need to be with others: fellowship, family, sexual intimacy etc.

Esteem covers less primal needs, achievement, respect, confidence and the like. With self-actualisation, we see our needs to solve problems, be creative and be good people.

Within the three layers I have proposed in Figure 14, the *Base* layer considers physiological and safety needs.

Let's think about a job for a moment. Most go to work for one reason, to earn money. Money leads to security. It provides you shelter, it keeps your family safe, it provides food for you all. Before money, jobs, and the like, this was all much more primal. You secured your family by physically protecting them. You hunted for food and you built shelters. For most, this is now taken care of by earning money. We do not need to hunt for food or build huts for shelter; we now buy all those things.

If we look at Maslow's hierarchy of needs again, we see the most core motivations for humans are physiological needs and safety/security.

Having just shown that now, money is what provides the majority of security for most; it makes sense that money is now one of our most core needs. I am not talking about being rich – rather having enough to guarantee physiological needs and safety.

Many people enjoy their job, which is great. Nevertheless, even those who say, "I would work here if they didn't pay me" are generally talking rubbish. You need to survive and in our world; work and money give you that opportunity.

Emotional / Intrinsic

Once our base needs and motivations are satisfied, we can focus on the other more emotional motivations. I describe these as our need for relatedness, autonomy, mastery and purpose (RAMP).

I will go into much more detail in the next section. These needs are referred to as intrinsic motivations and are much more important to our feeling of satisfaction than pure rewards can be.

Trivial / Extrinsic

A lot of gamification efforts sit in this area – often referred to as PBL gamification (Points, Badges and Leaderboards) [38]. They have their place and I will be explaining a lot more about them as we go along.

For now, it is enough to understand that these types of incentives are only truly effective when the first two layers of motivation and needs are satisfied.

It's always more complex than it looks!

As linear as this all seems, satisfy the bottom layer, then the middle, then use gamification, it isn't that simple. Short term engagement using extrinsic gamification can work fine, whatever the other needs may be, but it will have no sustainability. Also, what one person finds extrinsically motivating, others may find much more intrinsic.

The other key one to look at is Money in the base layer and Excess Bonuses being in the trivial/extrinsic section. Money is a base need these days, it is what helps us to guarantee security. Having more than we need is also not a terrible thing, money can't buy you happiness, but it can buy a lot of stuff that can go towards making you happy! However, there is a point where money is no longer the biggest interest. In a job you hate, you don't tend to leave because of the money, it is other factors. If you are then offered more money, it rarely makes you change your mind as the rest of the environment is the same! If you have enough money to be at least comfortable, then excess bonuses are not going to provide long-term motivation to do good work.

Excess bonuses can also lead to terrible behaviour, with overjustification effect being a massive issue. If you are just working for the money, quality can be affected as can decision making. Did you make the decision because it was best for the customer, or because it helped you get your bonus?

Using this in Gamification

The question becomes, how can we benefit from this knowledge in gamification? The answer is, by understanding what people need. Forget motivation for a moment and look at base needs. If a person feels they cannot support themselves and guarantee the security and safety of their family – no amount of emotional or trivial motivation is going to motivate them, at least not in the way you are probably hoping it will.

This is obviously focused on Enterprise gamification. It is not the job of an advertising company using gamification to sell a product, to ensure the base needs of their target audience. This is the job of the individual and their employer. However, if their target audience does not feel they have their base needs satisfied by work or other means, it is unlikely that the advertising will work on them, gamified or otherwise!

In the enterprise, be aware that if your employees are struggling financially and it is perceived that you could improve this, gamification could seriously backfire. The money you spend on that could be seen to be spent on improving the lives of the employees at a base level rather than a trivial one!

The Intrinsic Motivation RAMP

When creating your gamified solutions, it is important to find the intrinsic motivations that will keep your users engaged. Mastery is my main motivation, not that certain people would notice.

I have mentioned intrinsic motivation and extrinsic rewards a few times now, so it is about time to take a closer look at what they are and why an understanding of different types of motivation is so important.

Intrinsic motivation is defined by researchers Edward Deci and Richard Ryan as *"the doing of an activity for its inherent satisfactions rather than for some separable consequence"* [39]. They identify three intrinsic motivators: competence (or mastery), autonomy and relatedness which forms the core of their *Self-Determination Theory* [40].

In contrast, extrinsic motivation *is* *"a construct that pertains whenever an activity is done in order to attain some separable outcome"*

Daniel Pink's Drive [41], popular in gamification circles, suggests a slightly different set of intrinsic motivators. He proposes autonomy, mastery and purpose.

Comparing Self-Determination Theory and Drive

Self-Determination Theory	*Drive*
Competence	Mastery
Autonomy	Autonomy
Relatedness	
	Purpose

As you can see, the only real difference is that Pink drops relatedness for purpose, with mastery meaning the same here as competence.

Combining these four motivators, we get what I term the Intrinsic RAMP – Relatedness, Autonomy, Mastery and Purpose.

Intrinsic RAMP definitions

Motivation	*Description*
Relatedness	The desire to be connected to others.
Autonomy	The need to feel agency, independence or freedom.
Mastery	The desire to learn new skills and develop expertise in them.
Purpose	A feeling of greater meaning or a desire to be altruistic.

Intrinsic motivations are not perceived as a reward, either physical or virtual, but give people a feeling of satisfaction, sociability and self-determination. Every good gamified system will have one or more of these intrinsic motivators present in some form or another. This is not to say that extrinsic rewards are of no value, far from it. They can be a great way to reinforce and support motivation, as we will see later.

Relatedness

Relatedness is the desire to be connected to others. In gamification, social status and connections that come from communities satisfy this desire. I feel this is the glue that holds gamification together and elevates a gamified system above being just another gimmick. After the badges become boring due to habituation and the points are meaningless – having a community that enjoys their interactions with each other becomes the key to retaining their engagement and loyalty.

The sense of belonging and connectedness to other people is, in my mind, underrated. When you feel that you are part of a community and create relationships - that sense of community is much stronger than any digital reward you might get from posting an article to twitter!

Within the enterprise, this can be found in internal social networks as well as in the office. I mentioned social status as well. This may seem like an external force and to a certain extent, it is. However, status can be a very personal thing. Feeling that others value you, your input or your experience is very motivating. You do not need a leaderboard to feel that, you need to have connections with people and some way to get those people talking, sharing, and giving each other feedback.

Autonomy

Autonomy can have multiple meanings, but the core concept that I consider in gamification is that of freedom or agency. Most people do not like to feel that they are being controlled or stifled. Without some level of freedom, you will struggle to cultivate innovation and creativity.

As previously mentioned, Google recognised this when they implemented their 80/20 rule. Their employees were encouraged to spend 20% of their time working on their own projects. This led to some of their most important innovations, Gmail and Google News being two well-known graduates of this way of thinking!

You could also look at this in terms of meaningful choices. When teaching a new topic or idea, are you giving the user the freedom to choose how they learn for instance? Are they able to choose the path that best suits their needs or learning style or are they forced to do it one way or no way?

Giving users a level of autonomy will help them to feel that they have at least some control of what they are doing. For example, in an enterprise situation, it is the difference between micromanagement and leaving your employees to get on with their job. It shows them that they are trusted and can not only give you happier people but may also surface some great innovation.

Mastery

Mastery is the process of becoming skilled at an activity and eventually mastering it – becoming an expert. It is important to us that we feel our skill is increasing in direct proportion to the level of challenge. If this is perfectly balanced, it is often referred to as *Flow*, discussed later.

The path to mastery is an important concept seen in most if not all video games. These days, rather than being given a manual to read, you are guided through training levels that spoon-feed you everything that you need to know to master the game. This early phase is referred to as on-boarding.

The challenge is increased as your level of skill increases. Once you are out of the training levels, this does not cease. The game continues to get harder as you get better at it, but it offers less and less hand-holding.

In an enterprise situation, it is important to consider that if you do not continue to challenge employees, they will begin to feel less motivated. In the same way, if you do not encourage them to improve or even change their skills in ways that line up with their own desires, over time you will see de-motivation.

Purpose

When I speak about purpose in RAMP, I am specifically talking about **altruistic purpose**. This is the desire to help others in some way [42]. This is the type of purpose we are speaking of in the *Philanthropist* User Type.

The other type of purpose is **meaningful purpose**. This is more a desire to understand the meaning of what you are doing and our significance in the general scheme of things [43]. This type of purpose is experienced by all use types, it is not specific to one.

A very well-known example that encompasses both types of purpose is that of *Wikipedia*. Millions of articles, all given freely by people, for no other reason, than to feel that they may add to a better understanding of the topics [44].

More altruistic examples would be giving to charity, answering people's questions on forums like *Quora* or just opening the door for another person.

In the enterprise, you can implement this in a few ways. The first is giving people the ability to provide meaningful help to others. This links in well with relatedness when you look at internal social networks. Research has shown that altruistic actions can make people feel good about themselves – described often as a warm glow [45].

Another option is to give people the opportunity to give to charities from within gamified systems, especially in point collecting style platforms. For example, online quiz *Grain of Rice* asks players to answer questions. Each correct answer translates into donations of rice to countries suffering from famine.

So rather than giving users a badge, you should consider giving them the chance to donate to a charity of their choice when they hit certain thresholds.

Intrinsic motivation is important as it rewards people in a way that has a much deeper and more sustainable effect on people. However, that is not to say that extrinsic rewards are bad, they just need to be used smartly and in combination with intrinsic motivation and other drivers, not on their own. Gamification is all about getting the balance right!

It is also important to consider that RAMP is not a taxonomy, people are not one or the other, they are a spectrum of all the motivations, and much more! That said, depending on the context, one motivation may be more important to them than another.

For example, if generally a person is most interested in relatedness and you put them into an educational setting, at that moment mastery may be the most "active" motivation.

Learning from Games: Battlefield 1

Playing Battlefield 1 has reminded me how important the motivations I speak about in RAMP really are, but how they can be a little counter-intuitive at first glance.

Relatedness, Purpose and Goals

For instance, it becomes quickly apparent that teamwork is not initially facilitated by social connectedness/relatedness or communication, as you might expect. Rather it is created through the purpose provided by a common set of goals. This is especially true of playing on a public server with strangers!

Most players on each team want the same basic overarching goal – to win. To achieve this, they have capture control points. This is easier to achieve if you work together. To help you along, when the game starts you can join a squad. Each squad has a leader who can assign tasks. You don't have to do them but doing so can lead not only to better chances of winning but more experience points.

This creates a nice granular sense of purpose. First, there is the epic goal of beating the other team. Next, there is the more immediately achievable goal of capturing the next control point. After there are less obvious goals, like keeping your team alive and other players on your side.

Another key to success is choosing complementary character classes. This is not essential but can make a significant difference.

You can't rely on just being on the offensive all the time, people need healing and vehicles need repairing. Again, there is nothing forced, but it improves the chances of winning and the rewards that accompany winning. I'll get back to rewards in a moment, though.

Of course, the addition of voice communication, text communication and the ability to play with friends all add to the experience and increase the social feel of the game. I spent many hours playing Battlefield online with friends from Gamerdads over the years.

Mastery

Another more obvious motivation is mastery. Practice makes perfect, or so they say. As with most games, Battlefield pushes you to constantly improve. As you play you gain experience points. These are awarded for various actions in the game. Killing enemy players, rescuing teammates, capturing conquest flags, spotting the enemy for others, healing people etc. As you gain experience points, your rank increases. This is a very nice example of *continuous contextual performance feedback* (CCPF as I will now call it).

This helps you to understand how you are improving as well as what your key strengths are and can be easily seen at the main game screen. There are badges, but they are harder to earn – making them even more valuable and desirable over time.

To help you find a constant challenge, without pushing you too far beyond your current capabilities (expanded on later when discussing Flow), the server you are added to when you start a game is chosen with your current rank in mind. The algorithm tries to balance the teams based on ability so that there is a mix of players. Some a higher rank than you, some the same level as you and others maybe a little lower than you. This means that you are not just dying constantly, but neither are you likely to go totally unchallenged in a game.

Autonomy

That's Mastery and Purpose, both in terms of meaning and altruism (helping teammates, driving vehicles etc) fulfilled and even a little bit of Relatedness. But what of Autonomy? Well, each map is open, so you can roam wherever you like. You don't have to do anything that I have spoken about if you don't want to. There are always those who will play the game as a lone wolf, sniping from a distance or just charging into a fight and creating chaos (Disruptors). There no set path to follow and no set penalties for not following orders. There is some social pressure to at least work towards the same goals as the team and of course the potential desire to win, but that's about it. You really are a free agent.

Rewards – not always Evil!

It's not all about pure intrinsic motivation, though, Battlefield 1 makes good use of rewards as well. The more you play, the more experience points you get, the more currency you get, and the more unlockable options become available.

What I have always found interesting about this sort of system is that it seems a bit back to front when you think about it. The better you get, the better the weapons you can have. They become more accurate, more powerful, faster etc. Now, surely, these would make it much easier for new players to win games?

But that's the point. If new players could just come straight into the game with an elite weapon, they would never have to earn anything or learn the ropes. Giving new players too high an advantage from the outset will make them less appreciative of skill development and challenge.

Everything you unlock in Battlefield 1 makes you feel good because you worked hard to earn it. You also have the freedom to choose what you do and don't unlock. So, you may have got to the correct rank or completed specific tasks that allow you to open certain weapons, but you don't have to buy them. This adds to the feeling that you are playing the game how you want to play it.

There is much more here, random rewards, side missions and customisation to name a few, but what I have outlined are the things that have had me most engaged.

Again, this all hammers home the message that you need to cater for intrinsic motivations in your systems as well as the more obvious extrinsic ones. It also reinforces that rewards need to be earned not just given away, which I will expand on later.

What is Flow and Why is it Important?

When I train, often time seems to stop and there is nothing be me and the universe. This is the sense of Flow that my Master rattles on about all the time. Apparently, it is important in some way...

Flow and Happy Users

Flow is something you will hear a lot of in gamification and games for that matter. In gamification, it can help explain how to balance the user journey towards mastery.

Flow is a theory that was developed by Mihaly Csikszentmihalyi after seeing that under certain conditions, people's experiences became *optimal*. This is to say that they became totally focused on the job at hand. This can be seen in many artists who just "get into the grove" as they work, or athletes who are "in the zone" as they compete. Time stops, nothing else matters and when they finally come out of it, they have no concept of how long they have been doing what they were doing.

He identified some key factors that could lead to Flow: [46]

1. One must be involved in an activity with a clear set of goals and progress. This adds direction and structure to the task.
2. The task must have clear and immediate feedback. This helps the person negotiate any changing demands and allows them to adjust their performance to maintain the Flow state.
3. One must have a good balance between the perceived challenges of the task and their own perceived skills. One must have confidence in one's ability to complete the task.

The short version is that a person's perceived skill needs to match the perceived challenge, with clear goals and feedback. Well, as we will see – gamification is all about goals and feedback!

The model that Csikszentmihalyi suggested has more states than Flow – Flow is just the optimal state. If the challenge is low and the skill needed is low, then the user will be in a state of apathy. As the balance changes, the person can experience states of boredom, anxiety/frustration, worry and more.

The full model is shown in Figure 16. Most people spend much of their time somewhere in the middle.

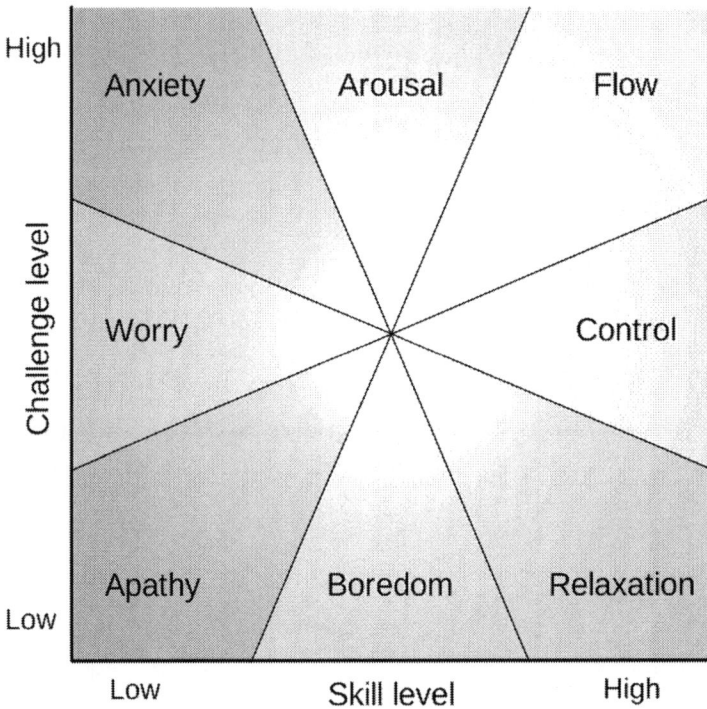

Figure 16 Flow: Challenge vs Skill

When we look at games, a variation of this model is often used – popularised in Jesse Schell's book *The Art of Game Design*.

In this simplified version, he concentrates on just three basic states: boredom, frustration and Flow.

During gameplay, it is usually preferable to keep a user within the "Flow Channel", the state between boredom and frustration. The closer the game takes a person to high challenge vs. high skill – the higher the state of Flow.

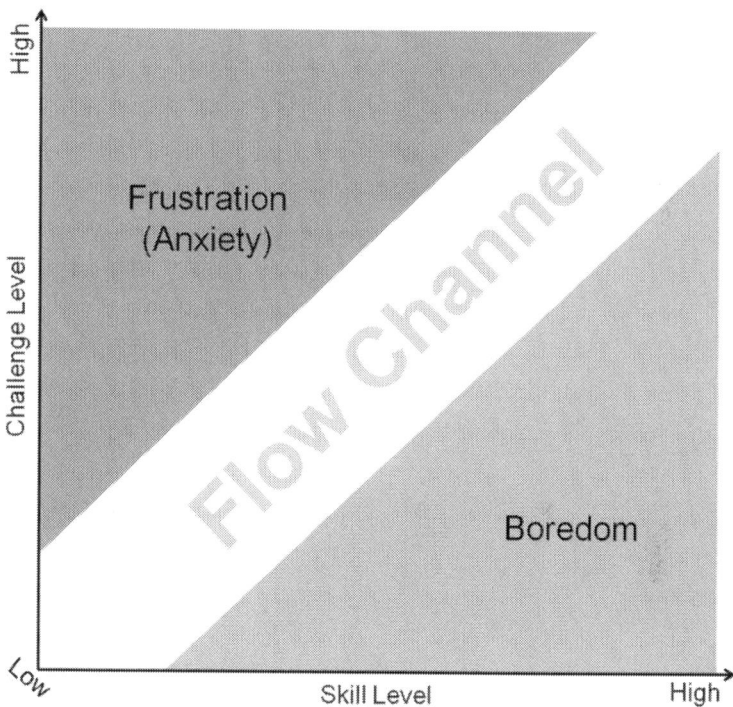

Figure 17 A Simplified View of Flow

It is important to explain that this is a snapshot in time, a representation of a person's state in a single moment.

When designing solutions, you must consider that people need to find the challenge evolves over time, in line with their skill. Increase the challenge before they are ready, and they will become frustrated. Keep the challenge constantly the same, they will master the skill and get bored, as with a game like *Tic Tac Toe*.

Take an admin job in a large company as an example. The employee starts on day one and with the relevant skills, but they probably need to learn about the company and learn how to use the skills in the way that is expected of them. If this happens too fast, their skills will not match the level of challenge and they will become frustrated.

We will look at the User Journey later in the book, however in gamification terms we would say that the *on-boarding* phase here is poor. Instead, you would create a system or process that enrolled the employee in a way that helped them understand how the company worked and how they integrated with it. This would be at a pace that was not too fast and not too slow.

For me, the ideal employee enrolment contains a few steps. The first is face to face. Truly, nothing can beat meeting people face to face to get to know them. So, start with a half day physical meetup that helps everyone become comfortable with each other. In that meeting, include core essentials that help them get started on their job. Where to find the timesheet software, how to get to the intranet, who their HR manager is, that sort of thing. After that, the rest can be handled with online courses and carefully planned drip-feeding of key information over the first days and weeks of their employment.

No one wants two days of *Death by PowerPoint*!

Figure 18 Death by Powerpoint

The challenge needs to keep going and increase as they learn new skills. There will often come a point where there is no way for their skills to increase and the challenge is no longer acceptable. Here there are two clear choices, move on or start to share that mastery with others.

What often happens at work when someone gets to this phase, is they are left to become bored and in turn, disenfranchised. This is when you lose employees. Never be afraid to allow them to move to new challenges if that is what it takes to keep them.

The lesson is, always make sure the skill and challenge levels are increasing in line with each other.

Grinding to Mastery and Flow

In game design and gamification design, we are also used to the idea that you "zig-zag" the user's skill with the challenge levels to keep users engaged and in the Flow "zone".

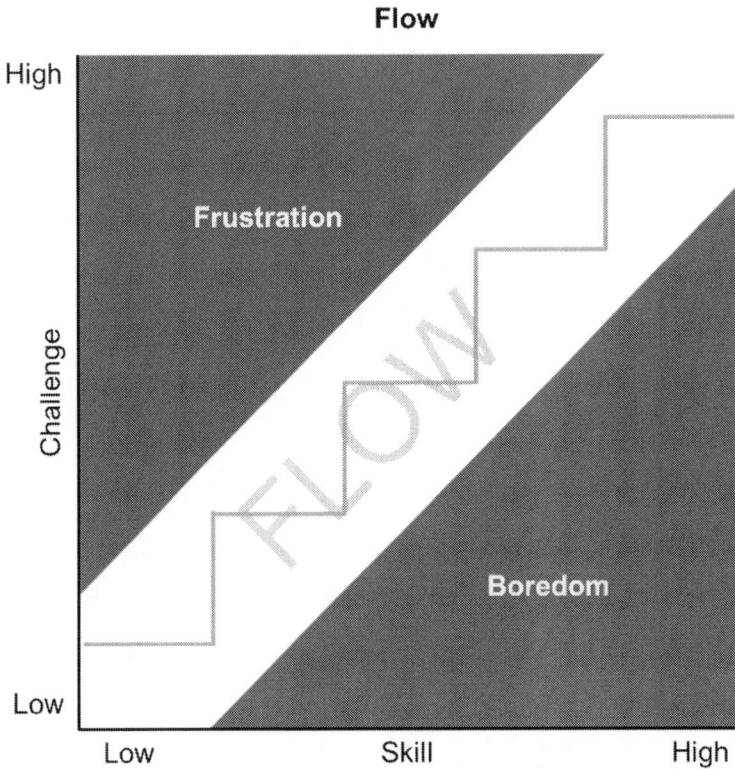

Figure 19 Ideal Flow

As we journey towards mastery, we go through several phases of activity in various combinations.

Phases

- **Grinding**: Low skill, low challenge work that is used to gain experience and increase skills.
- **Levelling**: As skills increase relative to the current challenge, the challenge levels increase.
- **Mastering**: The point where the user's skill levels match or surpass the challenge offered.
- **Testing**: Where the challenge is distinctly higher than the relative skill of the user. In games, this is often a Boss Battle. The user needs to "up their game".

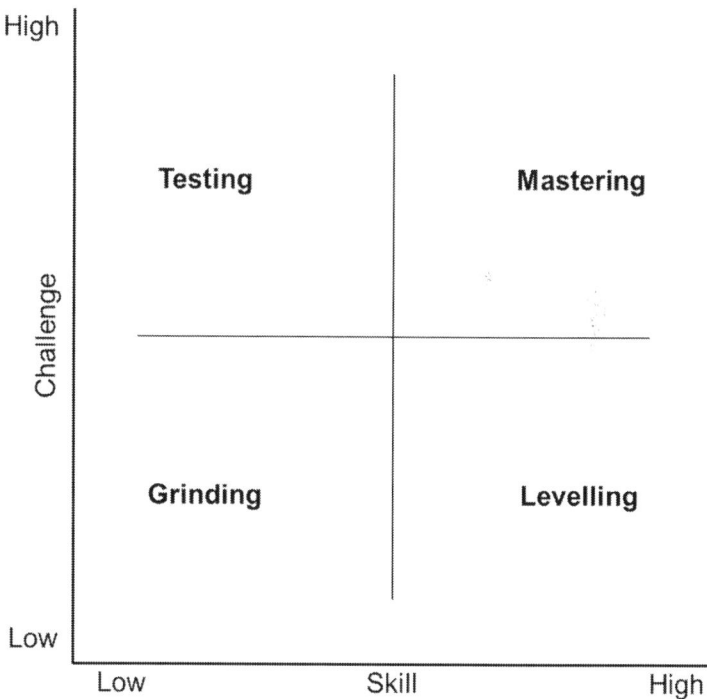

Figure 20 4 Phases

The Cycles

Grinding

The user has a low level of skill and is asked to complete simple challenges. As their skills increase and they start to "level up", eventually they will master that level of challenge. At this point, the challenge is increased, and they start grinding again. The challenge is now harder than when they started, but their skill has increased a relative amount, effectively resetting everything back to low skill / low challenge.

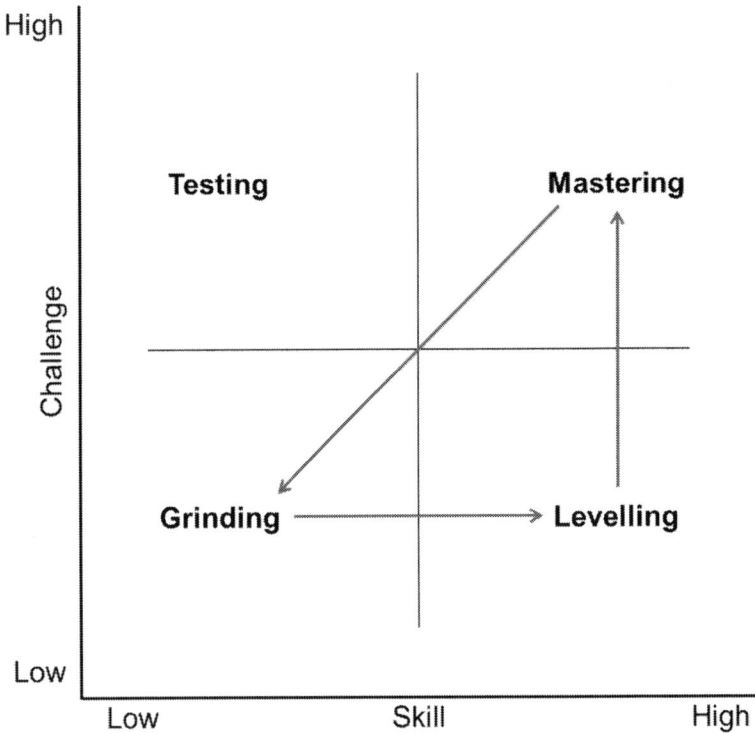

Figure 21 Grinding Cycle

Challenging

In this phase or cycle, there is an extra level of challenge in the form of a test. Mastering the current level of challenge leads to a display of skill against a higher challenge. In a game, you would see this as a boss battle. The player takes all they have learned and collected through grinding and applies it in a single much harder challenge. Usually, this will be a large spike in the challenge, but the reward for success would be greater!

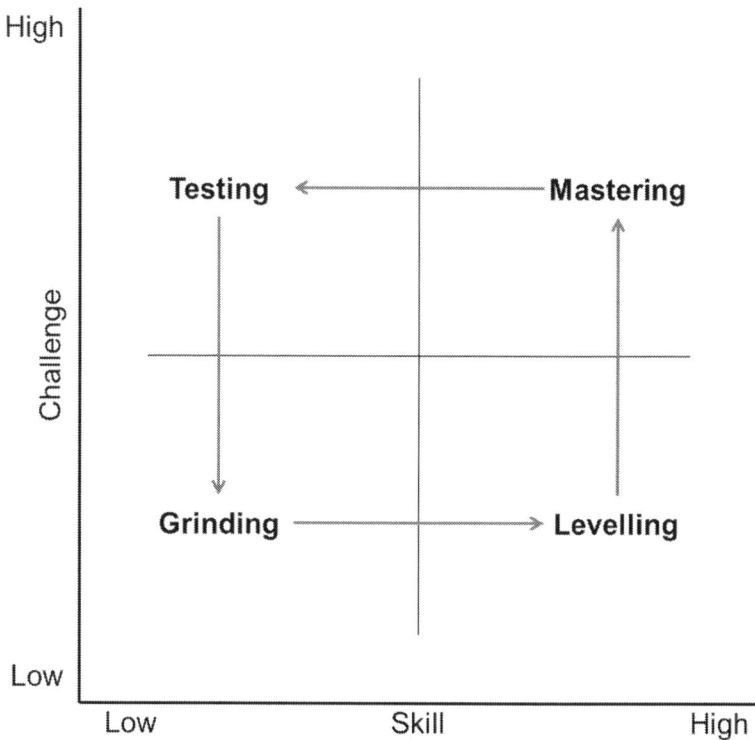

Figure 22 Challenging Cycle

Mastering

After a while, grinding is not enough to engage or entertain the highly skilled users, so one tactic is to keep the Boss Battles coming. Rather than resetting constantly to relative low skill / low challenge grinding, keep levelling, mastering and then testing the user. Eventually, this will cease to be entertaining though, they will out skill the system – then they can be considered the master of the whole system!

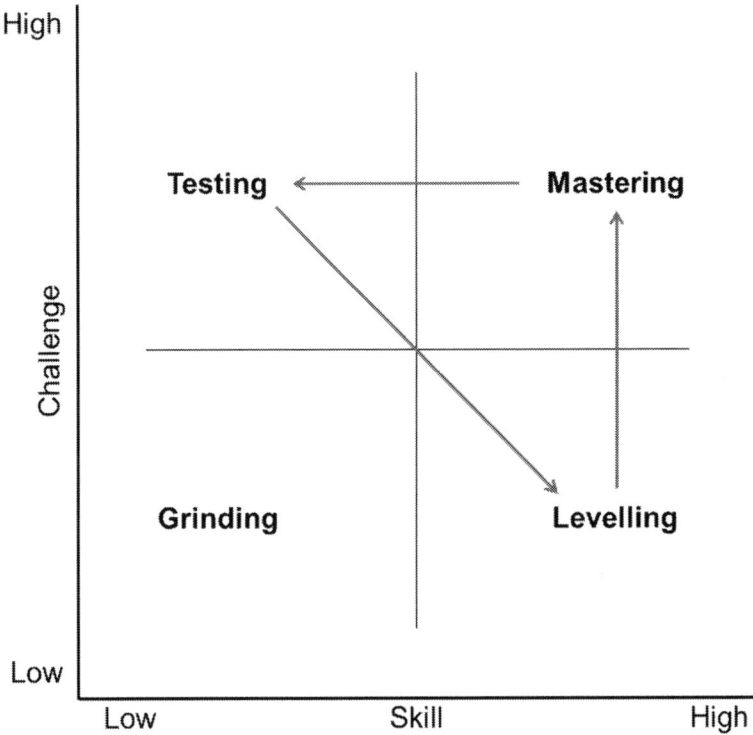

Figure 23 Mastering Cycle

Grinding to Flow

If we take all these cycles and apply them to our original Flow chart, we can see that each of these cycles can be repeated multiple times as the relative skill of the user increases. Flow is maintained by this repetition.

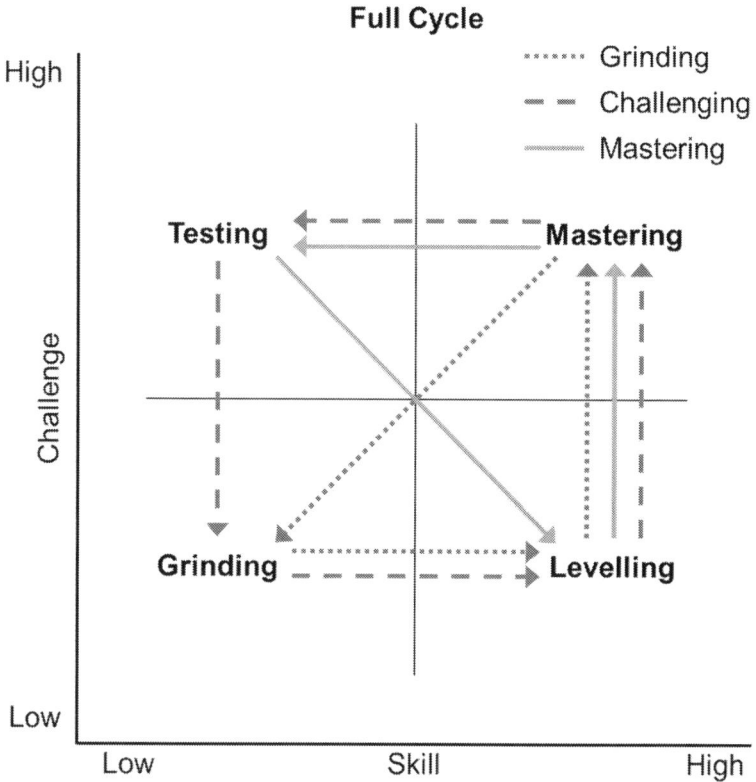

Figure 24 Grinding to Flow

The key is to keep the user out of the Boredom and Frustration areas as much as possible – but not be afraid to put them there from time to time. Grinding -> levelling can lead to boredom if you never give them anything to master. Continuously testing a user without allowing them to level up would lead to being constantly frustrated.

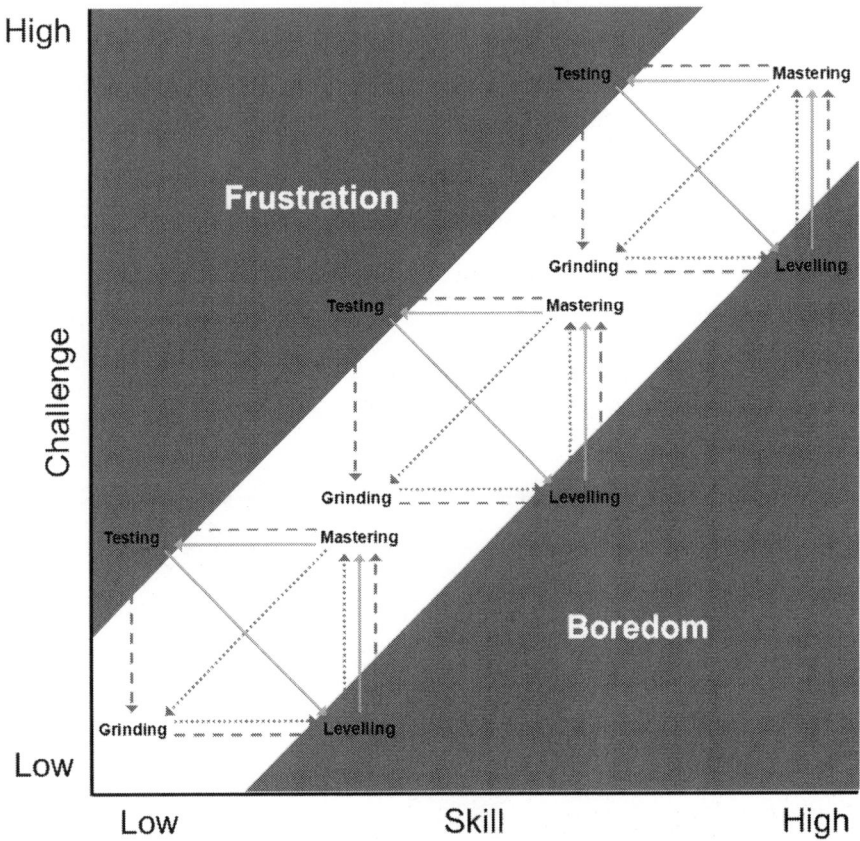

Figure 25 Grinding to Mastery

User Types in Gamification (The HEXAD)

So, my Master wasn't convinced that video game focused player types were a good fit for gamification.

Thinking he was clever, he created his own version – the User Type HEXAD. Yeah, whatever, but I do like the look of the Disruptor type.

Motivation brings us to one of my favourite topics – user types and player types!

In the games industry, player types are a well-known concept. Whilst there are many player type models and taxonomies out there, such as Amy Jo Kim's Social *Player Types* [47] or Chris Batemans's *Brainhex* [48], the most often quoted one is Dr Richard Bartle's Player Types [49].

By his own admission, Bartle's types are great for helping create MMO games, but they have little to no relevance when building gamified systems. As such, I created my own - Gamification User Types HEXAD.

Rather than being based solely on observed player or user behaviour, I initially created these types as personifications of our four intrinsic motivations (RAMP).

Before I take a proper dive into the types, it is essential to keep in mind that people cannot be broken down into simple individual categories like this. They will likely display most if not all of these traits in varying degrees [50].

When creating a gamified system, you need to design to encourage the behaviours that will give your system the best outcome, whilst engaging as many users as possible. These types can help with that.

In Brief

Socialisers are motivated by ***Relatedness***. They want to interact with others and create social connections.

Free Spirits are motivated by ***Autonomy*** and self-expression. They want to create and explore.

Achievers are motivated by ***Mastery***. They are looking to gain knowledge, learn new skills and improve themselves. They want challenges to overcome.

Philanthropists are motivated by ***Purpose and Meaning.*** This group are altruistic, wanting to give to other people and enrich the lives of others in some way - with no expectation of reward.

Disruptors are motivated by ***Change***. In general, they want to disrupt your system, either directly or through other users to force positive or negative change.

Players are motivated by extrinsic ***Rewards***. They will do what is needed to collect rewards from a system and not much more. They are in it for themselves.

The User Types HEXAD

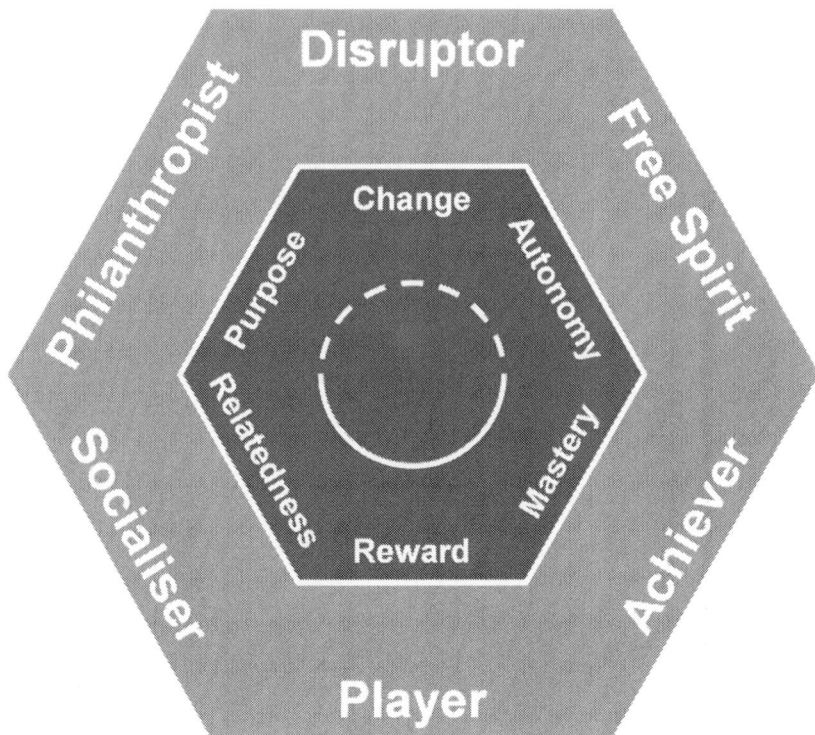

Figure 26 Marczewski's User Type HEXAD

These six types are enough to help most create engaging systems, however, if you want to get really into it – keep reading. Otherwise, jump to the next chapter!

For the rest of you, the User Types can be broken down into four intrinsically motivated types, four extrinsically motivated types (the Player) and four disruptive types (the Disruptor).

Intrinsic User Types

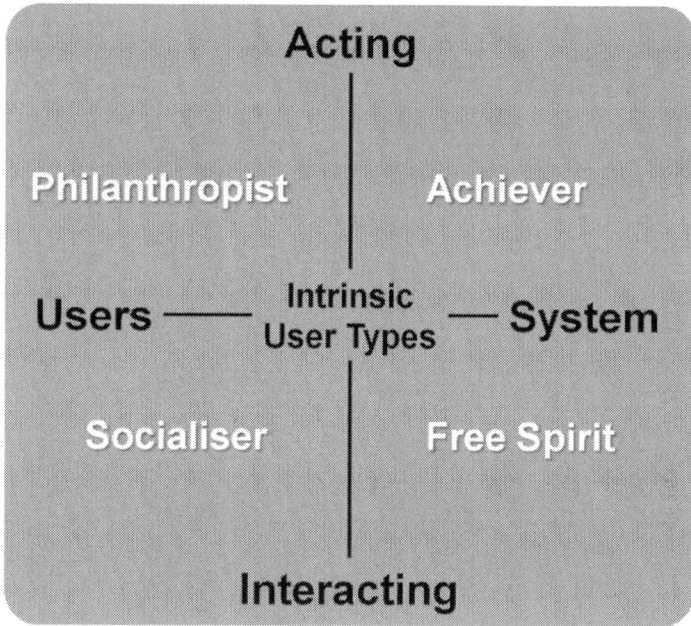

Figure 27 Intrinsic User Types

Philanthropists: This group are looking for a sense of purpose and meaning. For some this may be altruism, for others it may be more of a feeling that what they are doing serves some higher purpose. For example, users who contribute to Wikipedia often do so with no expectation of reward, they just wish to contribute to the collective knowledge of society [44].

Achievers: Typically motivated by mastery, you can expect achievers to want to complete every challenge your system has and be the best at each one. Whilst tokens of completion such as certificates and badges may be gratefully received, they are not going to be the reason achievers engage with the system.

In the same way, they may enjoy having other people within the system, but rather than looking for social connections, they will be viewed as new challenges to master.

Socialisers: Within a gamified system, people who are looking to create social connections are described as Socialisers. They would be motivated by systems that promote relatedness, like social networks.

Free Spirits: Free Spirits are primarily motivated by autonomy. Autonomy, in the context of the User Types, refers to freedom from external control. They welcome systems that allowed exploration or creativity.

Player (Extrinsic) User Sub-Types

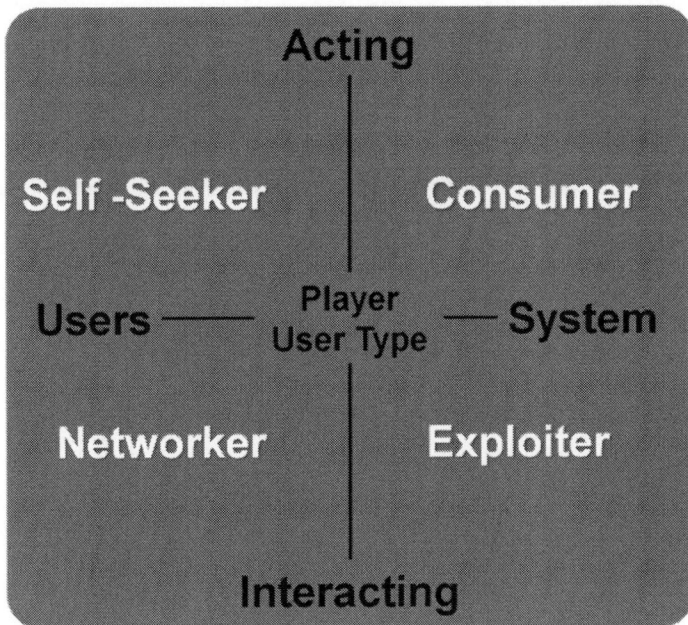

Figure 28 Player User Sub-Types

110

At their core, the Player user type is motivated by extrinsic rewards. They are the user type that will respond well to systems that offer points and badges as their core "game" elements. Within this type, there are several subtypes that behave in a similar way to the intrinsic user types to obtain the rewards on offer.

Self-Seeker: This group of users will act in a similar way to Philanthropists. They will answer people's questions, share knowledge and be helpful – but for a price. If there is no reward, do not expect them to get involved! They can be useful when quantity is more important than quality.

Consumer: Consumers will modify their behaviours to get rewards. If that requires them to learn new skills or take on challenges, like an Achiever, then they will do it. However, if they can get rewards for just doing the bare minimum – even better. Think of them as the ones who will enter competitions just for the prize or who shop at one store just for the loyalty programme.

Networker: Where a Socialiser connects to others because they are looking for relatedness, Networkers are looking for useful contacts from whom to gain something. They follow the big influencers on social networks, not because they are interested in them but because they hope it will get them noticed, increase their influence and lead to reward. They probably love *Klout (R.I.P) or Kred!*

Exploiter: Like Free Spirits, these people are looking for the boundaries of the system, where they can go and what they can do. However, for them, it is a way to find new ways to rewards.

If they find a loophole, do not expect them to report it unless they feel others are earning more than them exploiting it!

They are the most likely to exploit the system, some would even describe them as cheats. They are also the people who will build objects just to sell. Think of *Second Life*. Many people started to build custom items and objects, but some realised that as well as being fun, they could make some money from selling items. For a few this turned into a way of making a living [51]. They stopped making things for fun and just made them for profit.

The Player User Type is important to recognise, as most people coming into a gamified system are likely to enter initially due to rewards (points, prizes etc.). The trick is to try to convert them from being reward oriented into intrinsically motivated users (Socialiser, Free Spirit, Achiever, and Philanthropist).

There is some evidence in work done by Herbert Et Al [50] to show that the extrinsic types will convert to their analogous intrinsic types. For example, a Networker may convert to a Socialiser over time, but it is not a certainty in all cases. Design for the intrinsic user types that benefit your system but include reward paths in the on-boarding process for best effect and greatest coverage.

Disruptor User Sub-Types

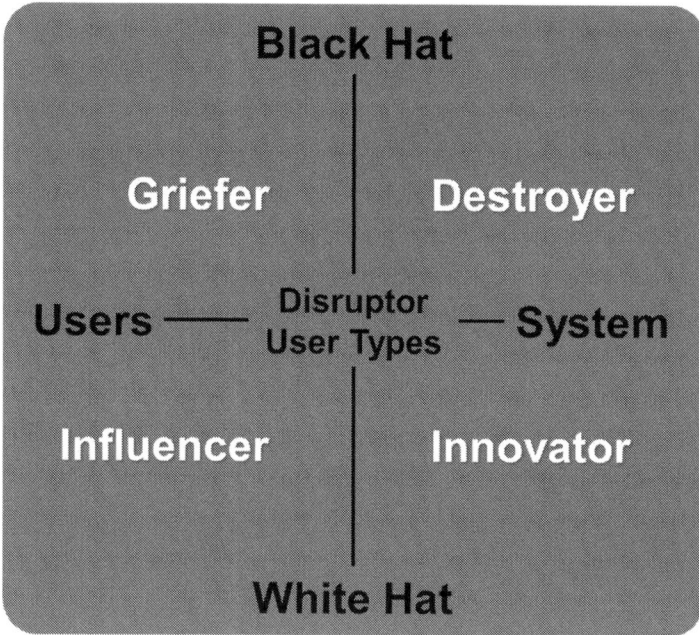

Figure 29 Disruptor User Sub-Types

Disruptors disrupt a system, positively or negatively, in some way. This may be by acting on users or on the system itself. As with the Player type, the Disruptor type is a group rather than a single type. However, I do not tend to go into the detail, as the effect on your design is generally the same for all the variations of the type.

Going into a deep dive, we get these four main types of Disruptor:

Griefer: This is straight out of Bartle's expanded eight types. I have chosen to use Bartle's description because this is the pure bully type. If you have ever heard of the Triad (or indeed Tetrad) of Dark Personalities [52] – these guys will tick one or all of the boxes!

113

They want to affect other users negatively, just because they can. It may be to prove a point about the fact they do not like the system, it may just be for fun. They have no place in most gamified systems, so you need to find ways to either change their minds – or get rid of them.

Destroyer: This type of user wants to break the actual system directly. This may be by hacking or finding loopholes in the rules that allow them to ruin the experience for others. Their reasons, again, may be because they dislike the system, or it may just be that they find it fun to hack and break stuff. If you cannot convince them to convert to an Improver, then you must get rid of them.

Influencer: These users will try to change the way a system works by exerting influence over other users in much the same way as a political leader might. This is not to say they are a negative type, far from it. If they feel the system needs to change and you allow them a voice to help change it, they could become massive advocates. Make use of them or you will lose them – worse still they could end up switching to a Machiavellian style Griefer!

Innovator: Innovators will interact with the system with the best intentions in mind. They may hack it or find loopholes, but their aim is to change the system for the better. They are like the Free Spirit type in reality; they want to have the chance to explore the system, find problems and try to fix them. A simple example would be those who submit support tickets for bugs and track their progress. Take care of these users as they can help you massively. Mistreat them and they may well become Destroyers.

As you can see, the Disruptor can be a complex type and although they make up a very small percentage of the overall user group, they can be very powerful. Handled correctly, they could help improve your system, handled badly, they may destroy it.

The Dodecad of User Types

The Dodecad is a visual summary of the 12 user types. If you look at the chart, closer to 12 o'clock and 6 o'clock are the Player user types. 9 o'clock and 3 o'clock are the disruptors and the rest are the intrinsic types.

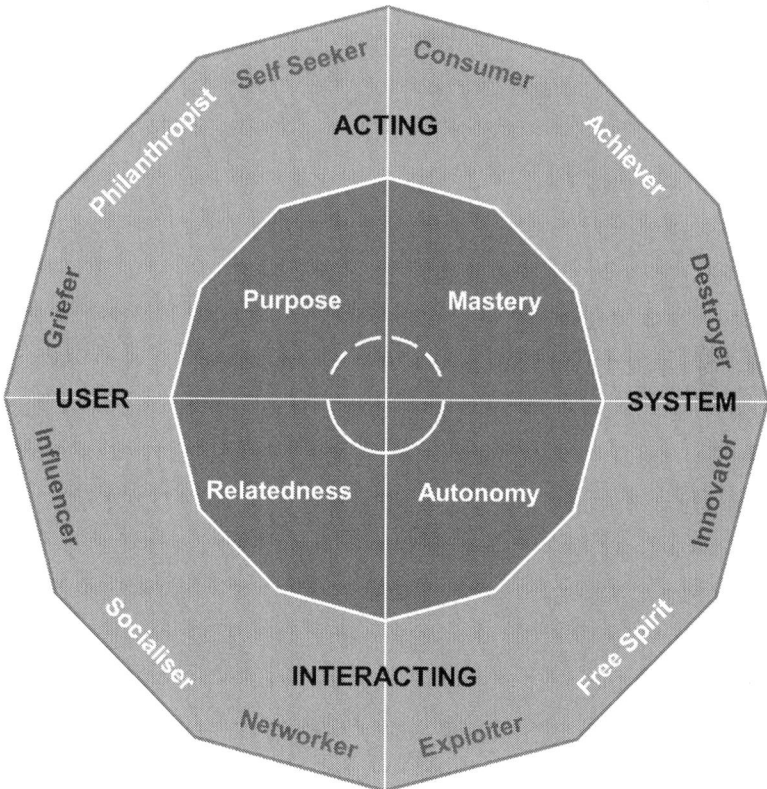

Figure 30 The Dodecad of User Types

Using the User Types

The HEXAD is a simple framework to look at basic motivations of users who are in your system. There are three main ways to go about using the user types in the early phases of your design.

Survey the Populous

The first option is to survey your intended target audience to find out what types they are. Then you can design a system that focuses mostly on those majorities.

Although surveying is a reasonable thing to do, it does have a couple of drawbacks. It assumes the questions are relevant. It requires people to self-report with honesty, something that we intend to do, but at times, we do not recognize that cognitive biases can prevent this from happening [53].

The final and most important drawback is the nature of people themselves. You see, the survey provides snapshot of information on the type for a potential user before they interact with the system and out of context. Over time it has been found that the user types can change [50]. The user type you are when you first start using a system may not stay the same. Therefore, surveying and building your system based on initial types may be counter-productive.

This is the approach if you are looking for a short-term campaign; you just need to work out what your potential users want over the immediate term.

Design Gamification for Types

An alternative is to come at designing for gamification types from another direction. Define the problem your gamification is trying to solve. Next work out what user types are most likely to be able to help solve it – and build the system to encourage and support them.

For instance, if you are looking for innovation in your company and you want to get people to submit new ideas, what types of people are most likely to give up their time to do this? Well, initially it would make sense that Philanthropists would be up for the challenge. Their "joy" comes from helping others and adding to the greater meaning of life the universe and everything.

This being the case, you need to create an environment that allows them to give their ideas, but also to advise others and support them with their ideas. You may also want to consider Free Spirits. They are creative and could be the ones who have explored areas where there can be the most innovation. This means you would create a system that encourages and supports their involvement. You give them tools to think creatively and develop their ideas.

That is not to say you ignore the other types. You can create social networking opportunities for Socialisers or add voting systems with points and badges for the Players (and Disruptors).

However, remember they are not the ones who will be helping you directly solve your problem. Also, remember that different motivations appeal to people in varying degrees and combinations.

117

Although they may be a Socialiser, they can still have traits that a Philanthropist may have.

This approach will help you build a system that solves your problem. Yes, users may evolve their type during usage, but the system will still encourage others to come along and use it. In addition, designed well, you can keep the evolved users on board in other capacities.

User Type Lenses

This is my personal favourite way of using the user types. The basic idea is to put yourself in a different position to view a problem from a different perspective. Based on the idea of a deck of lenses, stolen from Jesse Schell, each one challenges you to ask certain questions about your design to try and get a new perspective on it.

Disruptor
Change / Innovation / Disruption

* What can I break?
* Who can I upset?
* What can I improve / change?
* How can I be heard?

Free Spirit
Autonomy

* Can I be creative?
* Can I find my own way?
* Is exploration encouraged and rewarded?
* What is there to find?

Achiever
Mastery / Competence

* What will challenge me?
* How can I learn new skills?
* What will I have to show for at the end?
* How do I succeed?

Player
Extrinsic Rewards

* What's in it for me?
* How do I win?
* What's the easiest way?
* How do I need to behave to get what I want?

Socialiser
Relatedness

* How can I connect to others?
* Can I play with friends?
* How can I collaborate?
* How will I be recognised by my peers?

Philanthropist
Altruistic Purpose

* How can I help others?
* How can I share with others?
* How can I improve the experiences of others?

As you design your solutions, keep asking the questions on these cards to constantly evaluate what you are building and how it will appeal to different users. Later in the book, there is an outline of more than 50 mechanics and elements that can be used to support and encourage each of the six main user types.

The Neuroscience of Gamification

Brain chemistry is not the sort of thing I would usually
be interested in. However, it is useful to understand the
basics to cut through a lot of the hyperbole out there. I
like cutting through things.

One of the aims of this book is to give you the building blocks to hold your own in gamification. In gamification, there is often a lot of mention of concepts like "Neuroscience", "Neurochemistry", "Neurotransmitters" or "Brain Chemistry". In particular, you will hear people speak about neurotransmitters such as Dopamine (can you remember where I mentioned it?).

Neurotransmitters are chemicals that transmit signals around the brain. They all have different functions and have different effects on us. In this section, I am going to discuss four: **Dopamine**, **Oxytocin**, **Serotonin** and **Endorphins** (DOSE).

I am not even going to pretend to be an expert in this, but I wanted to present a few things here that you should know about and more importantly, know what they do. What I have outlined here are by no means the full functions of these neurotransmitters, merely the functions we are interested in with regards to gamification.

This is all researched and validated with the wonderful Andrea Kuszewski to make sure it is as accurate as possible for you.

Dopamine

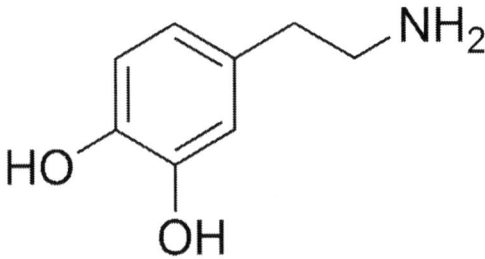

Figure 31 Dopamine

When I first started investigating gamification, everyone was talking about dopamine. It was considered the "pleasure" drug in the brain. Getting a reward, such as a digital badge, was thought to release dopamine which gave you pleasure. It turns out this is not actually quite right.

Dopamine has many functions, but I only want to talk about a couple that have relevance to us in gamification.

Motivation: It is released before an event that requires some sort of response, pleasurable or otherwise, and drives us to act. So when it comes to a reward, dopamine is released in anticipation of receiving the reward, rather than after [54]. This is known as incentive salience.

Learning: It is thought that dopamine plays a major role in associative learning, forming associations between an action or activity and its consequences [55].

Andrea Kuszewski puts it rather nicely [56]:

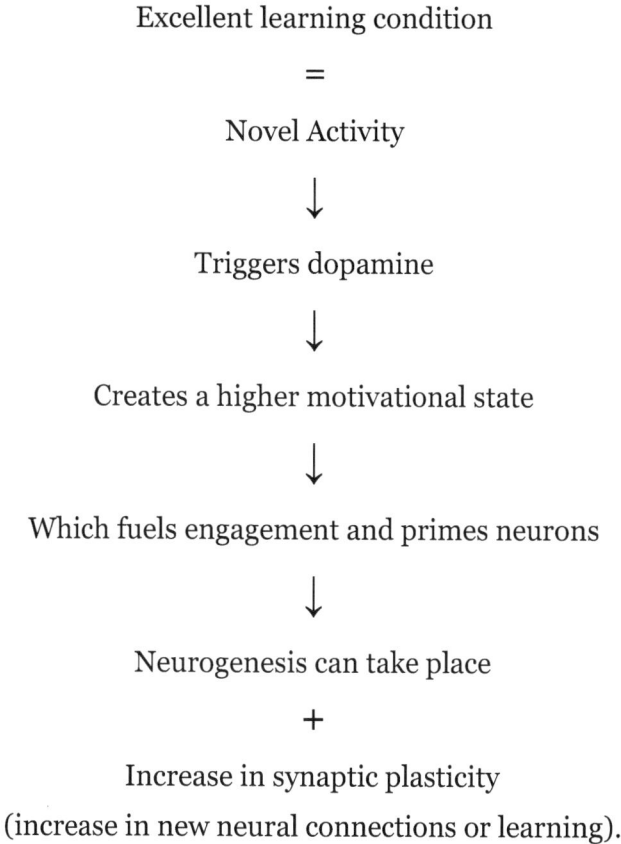

Excellent learning condition

=

Novel Activity

↓

Triggers dopamine

↓

Creates a higher motivational state

↓

Which fuels engagement and primes neurons

↓

Neurogenesis can take place

+

Increase in synaptic plasticity
(increase in new neural connections or learning).

Gamification to Increase Dopamine

New and novel experiences trigger dopamine (novelty as mentioned above). So, create systems that allow discovery and exploration. Your Free Spirit user types will enjoy this! Anticipation of potential rewards is another way, so creating manageable goals (think SMART Goals) can help. Andrea wrote a series on the role of dopamine and oxytocin in sex and pleasure.

The third part of the series concentrates on how ambiguity, suggestion and so on can increase pleasure [57]. It is worth keeping this in mind with your systems.

Oxytocin

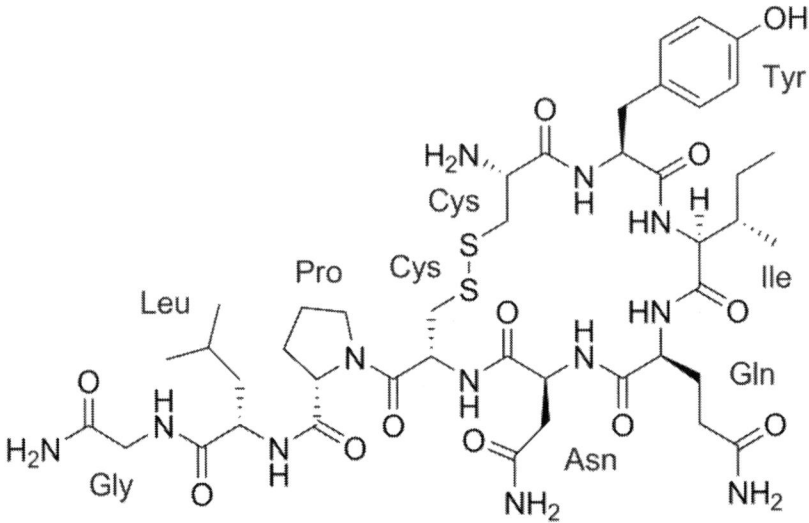

Figure 32 Oxytocin

Oxytocin is key to how we bond to others (mothers to babies, lovers, friends etc.). It can give us a strong feeling of contentment. Studies have shown that this can even occur remotely, with Paul J. Zak suggesting that using social networks like Twitter can create a similar reaction to falling in love! [58]. Oxytocin has also been shown to increase trust in groups, altruism in individuals, arousal, bonding and much more.[59]

However, there is another side to this. Previously thought to promote only the nicer side of social bonding, strengthening your feelings and reactions in social situations may not always be positive. In reality, it could lead to strengthening feelings of anger and dislike depending on the situation. [60,61]

Gamification to Increase Oxytocin

Interestingly, oxytocin is released when we are engaged with a strong narrative. This would seem to be part of why stories are more memorable than just pure facts (or dull PowerPoints!). It accounts for that feeling presence as you feel empathy towards the situations in the story [62].

Actually, and this is a slight tangent, stories affect our brains as if we were experiencing the events ourselves – worth remembering that!

Add social aspects to your system. As mentioned above, using platforms like twitter can create bonds and feelings as strong as falling in love. Socialiser types will love it.

Create a system that allows for altruism, giving to others selflessly can help create bonds and will release oxytocin – this is what the Philanthropist type lives for!

Also – go and hug someone – seriously!

Serotonin

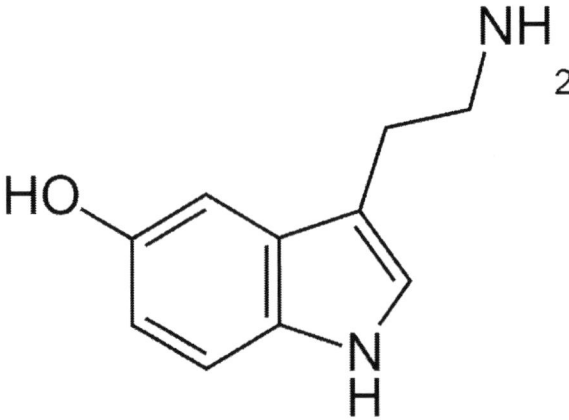

Figure 33 Serotonin

Serotonin is a mood regulator. If you have enough you will be happy if you don't – you will be miserable (put very simply!)[63]. It is triggered when you feel wanted, important and proud. This could be when you are thanked or have achieved something that required true effort. When people feel that they are unappreciated or worthless, they will have low serotonin levels.

Gamification to Increase Serotonin

Make sure your system records achievement in some way, even if it is badges. Serotonin release can be triggered by remembering past experiences where you felt wanted or important. Having badges or trophies that remind users of past success and the pride they felt at the time can do this. Also, give users the ability to thank each other in some way. This could be simple "thanks", "like" button or a system of kudos like stars and voting.

You could set up a system where you can send virtual gifts as thanks, also potentially triggering oxytocin release for the giver – another big hit with the Philanthropist types. Anything that makes your users feel wanted and important to you and other users.

Endorphins

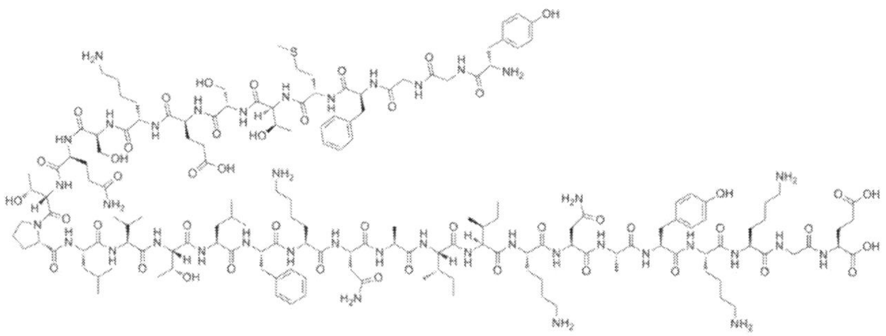

Figure 34 Beta-endorphin

Endorphins are opioids that we produce naturally as a reaction to certain stimuli. When they are released, we feel good. It can be a lot stronger than that, we can feel high or euphoric – in fact, it is very similar to morphine.

They also reduce fatigue in response to stress, or indeed pain, giving us our "second wind" that helps us push through. It is what gives runners the ability to keep going when they think they are done for physically [64]. It is also released during less physical activities – such as video games.

Overcoming the challenges in games can stimulate the release of endorphins, making gamers feel better about themselves and giving a sense of achievement [65].

Gamification to Increase Endorphins

The easiest way to stimulate endorphin release with gamification is to create situations where your users will feel they have achieved something. Rather than giving rewards for clicking buttons, you need to create challenges that require skill and effort to complete. If they feel they have worked hard, they will get that feeling of fiero, an epic win and with luck a hit of endorphins. The Achiever and Player types will love this!

There are many other neurotransmitters that could be discussed here, such as endocannabinoids and their involvement in motivation [66], however, these four give you enough to get going.

The point of knowing any of this is to understand that gamification can be used to influence mood and behaviour at a chemical level in the brain – making it very powerful if done properly and potentially harmful if you get it wrong.

User Types and Neurotransmitters

- Achiever (Mastery): Endorphin, Dopamine
- Socialiser (Relatedness): Oxytocin, Serotonin
- Philanthropist (Meaning/Purpose): Dopamine, Oxytocin, Serotonin
- Free Spirit (Autonomy): Dopamine
- Player (Rewards): Dopamine, Endorphin, Serotonin

BUILDING GAMIFIED SOLUTIONS

How to Start with The User Journey

I have been on a journey of learning for a long time now and it is my time to be the Master. Here you will find a journey of several phases explained. I am well and truly out of the Enthuse and Engage phases. My End Game? My *Master* will find out soon.

The Player Journey is a concept that I came across from the wonderful Amy Jo Kim. She talks about the player journey in terms of three main phases. On-boarding, Habit Building and Mastery [67]

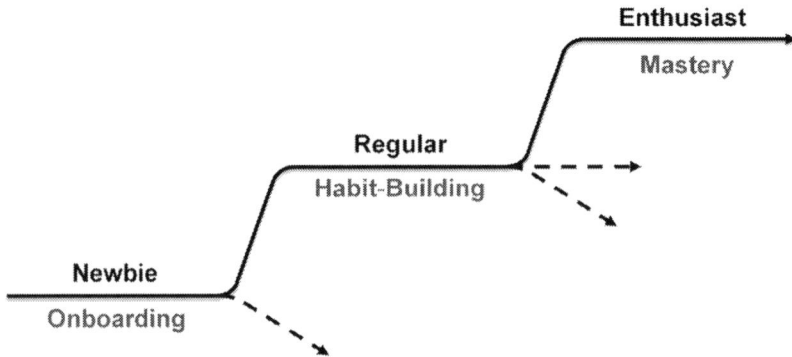

Figure 35 Amy Jo Kim's Player Journey

Over time, these are the main phases a player goes through whilst engaged with a game. They begin the path as a Newbie, orienting to the system they are entering. During the habit-building phase, they start to integrate the system into their specific situation or circumstances.

Eventually, they reach a level where there is no longer an increasing challenge and they will have mastered the material or system.

The same is true for users going through a gamified system. Users enter the system and must learn how to use it. Then they need to start using it day to day and finally, once they have mastered the system they will probably need something more.

As gamification and games are not quite the same and based on some of my experiences, I created a slight variation, called the Gamification User Journey.

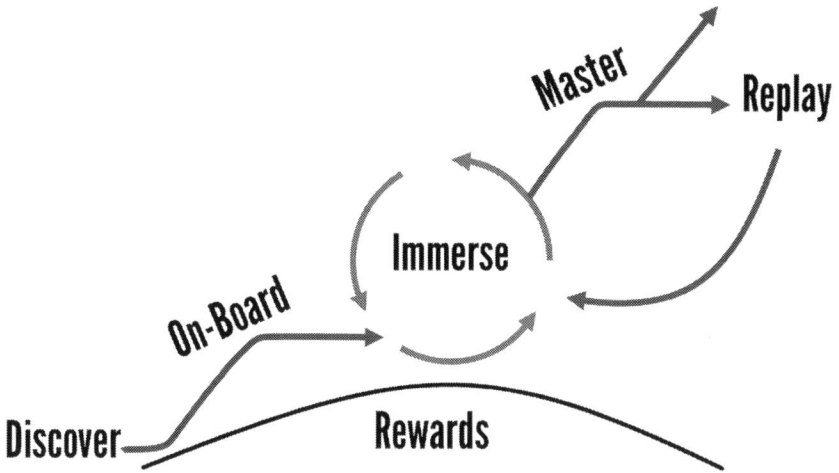

Figure 36 Gamification User Journey

Discover

There must be a discovery phase, like the attract screen in the arcades, because without it – how will people start to use the system? It may just be an email to tell you to do some mandatory training, it may be subtle posters that hint at something new. However, you decide to do it, it is essential and must fit with the overall theme of the programme.

On-board

Nothing new here, this is the scaffolding of the whole show. If you get this wrong, people will not get any further in their journey! It has the potential to be a massive drop off phase of the journey. You must balance it just right, to hold the user's hand enough to keep them going, but not so much they feel babied and foolish. Measured use of rewards can be of great benefit in this stage as digital "pats on the back".

Immerse

Once they are in the system and know what they are doing, they can immerse themselves in the activities – be it learning, day to day sales entry or any other activity. This is where good activity and feedback loops are essential to keep people engaged. It is also the stage of the journey where you will need to stop relying on rewards and start helping the users find their intrinsic reason to be there.

Master

This is the phase where a couple of things may happen. This may be the point where the journey ends, the user has finished and has met the end-game requirements, game over man... However, it may also be the start of the next phase of the journey, a bit like the Black belt in martial arts. You have mastered the first journey, now you must move on to the second and third etc. *Achievers* aim for this level and will work hard to get it. Make sure they feel rewarded for their efforts (and I don't mean points and badges!!!)

Replay

If there is no specific moment where the journey ends, you need to include replayability. This can come in several forms. It could be an opportunity for the ones who have completed, to try and ace it. Think about casual games where you can finish a level with 1, 2 or 3 stars. The replay value comes from trying to get through levels you didn't score 3 on again, trying to attain the maximum.

It may be that they get to play again at a high difficulty – remember the Nightmare mode from Doom? It may be that they can play again with a different role.

In the case of a learning related system, they could go back with the role of master, rather than apprentice, acting as a guide and mentor to those who are yet to master the earlier phases. You can really leverage the Philanthropist User Types here.

Figure 37 The Gamification User Journey

How to Use Points, Badges and Leaderboards

Winning is in my DNA. I am motivated by being the best, but a reward every now and again is always appreciated, at least, it would be if I ever got one. Even a pat on the back would be nice.

In contrast to intrinsic motivation, extrinsic motivation is all about the rewards. Deci and Ryan define this as

"a construct that pertains whenever an activity is done in order to attain some separable outcome" [39]

In terms of gamification, these are considered as any reward that is given to a user as an incentive to behave in a certain way or complete actions. Examples would be points, badges or leaderboards (PBL). As you saw in the last chapter, I refer to the users who engage best with systems focusing on extrinsic rewards as Players.

Common examples of gamification often concentrate on these three simple game-like elements, often with unintended results. You often find them on websites looking to increase user engagement. Sadly, these implementations are often poorly thought out and designed.

First, let's explore the use of these. There is no denying that when you are building a gamified solution, at least one of these is going to turn up at some point, so it is best to understand them and understand their uses and limitations.

Points

Giving points is a simple enough concept. In video games, points are often given to players for completing certain tasks. Kill the bad guy, find the scroll, save the prince or princess. In gamification, this is frequently translated into completing less enjoyable tasks. Press the "Like" button, leave a comment and use the same shop multiple times.

Points help to power progress tracking, reward management, badges, achievements, leaderboard position and more. Even if the end user never sees them, most systems have some form of points running in the background.

Points can come in several forms such as Experience Points (XP), virtual currency, stars, kudos and so on. Whatever they may be called, at their core they are all types of feedback.

Virtual Economy

Points can be seen as a type of currency on their own. In a way, you are paid in this virtual currency for undertaking actions that the system has asked you to engage in. However, it is possible to take that a step further. You could create an economy where it is possible to buy, sell and trade using the virtual currency. Virtual economies can be based entirely in the virtual world or can break that barrier and have some effect on the real world, depending on how they are designed.

Many games allow you to collect coins or points and then exchange them for in-game goods. An example that I have been playing recently is *Fallout: Shelter* from Bethesda. As you play the game, you earn bottle caps – the in-game currency. Those bottle tops can then be used to purchase new rooms for your shelter. This is a self-contained virtual economy. You play the game and do the deeds asked of me, earn virtual money and spend it in the virtual shop.

However, if you wish to speed up the process, you can use real money to purchase more bottle caps.

At this point, the virtual economy can be influenced by the real world. This is something that social games like *Farmville* have been doing very well for some years now.

Another way for the real world to influence the virtual economy is the sale of virtual goods for real money. As I mentioned previously, *Second Life* produced a real world millionaire, Anshe Chung [51], through the sale of virtual property for real money!

All of this can be done in gamification, but you have to consider some of the legal ramifications that go with economies that affect the real world as the rules can vary – especially around using virtual currency as a replacement for real currency [68].

As an example of how this may work in gamification, consider a software company. They have a base product that is free to use. Additional functionality can be purchased as and when it is required. In games, this is often referred to as *freemium*. The basics are free, but extras cost. They want to create a loyalty scheme where users of the free software can earn points that can be traded for time-limited upgrades.

In this situation, you could set up a system where a desirable action, such as sharing a link to the software or helping others in a forum earns the user points. Points are then converted into virtual currency and that virtual currency can be used to purchase these upgrades.

You must decide how much effort each of these upgrades is worth and then convert the points earned in a sensible way. For instance, if the upgrade is worth $20, you do not want to give it away to someone just for one share!

giffgaff, a mobile network provider, do exactly this with minutes. Supporting other users on the forum earns you minutes that can be used on your mobile phone [69].

Badges

Badges and trophies are the next level of feedback in a system. They represent particular achievements. In games, you will see them being given for displays of skill such as long-distance shots, kill streaks, and finding secrets.

In gamification, they are more likely to be used to say well done for repeated activities and their related achievements. Liking 100 articles or being loyal to a service provider for an extended period, that sort of thing. Done well they can represent anything from social status to competency and carry purpose and meaning to the users who *earned* them.

Try to make badges fun, both graphically and in their meaning. Getting a new badge for every 10 shares gets old very fast. Try to find *fun* ways to assign them. As you have seen, I like to include rewards that relate to 42 where I can – *Hitchhikers Guide to the Galaxy* fans will know why. My other favourite is to give badges for 11 actions (look into *Spinal Tap* – it goes to 11). Surprise people and make them laugh. Make them work and have badges that require exploration and imagination.

Not all badges have to be given automatically; you can set ones up that are assigned by peers. When a member of an online forum is helpful, other users of the forum give them a badge that thanks them and commends them for being so helpful. Not only does this have more meaning to them, it shows other users that they can go to them for help! Many forums use a system of Karma points for exactly this. Another benefit is that it can help to highlight high-value users to admin and other users.

As people become more involved with a system, there is a point where you cannot just keep giving endless badges and expect users to continue to be engaged. If your system wants to encourage long-term usage, it must have more than badges to keep people going. You can add new badges as you go along, but that can become problematic. It is time-consuming and hard to keep creating inventive and interesting badges. You also must be careful that the ones you add do not devalue ones that are already there.

This happens either when you make a badge easier to earn or if a more valuable badge is added to the system and is relatively easier to earn than previous badges.

Badges in Education

In education, they can be used very effectively as a way of representing academic achievement as part of a personal record in systems such as *Moodle*. Rather than just relying on grades, experiences points leading to academically related badges can be implemented to help students track their progress in a more granular and real-time way. It doesn't even need to be a full learning management system.

Education and gamification expert Alice Keeler makes amazing use of Google spreadsheets to manage everything from gamified peer assessment to personal development plans [70].

Check off with an X	Level	★	XP	Agenda Item Number	Title	Description	Badge	Link
					You are Level 3			
X	1	☆	10	1	Let's Do This	Log Into Google Account		
X	2	★★	5	2	I Made This	Create a Google Doc from Google Drive		http://drive.google.com
X	2	★★	10	3	You're My Friend	Name and Share the Google Doc		
	3	★★★	15	4	Box Me In	Insert a table and right click to choose table properties. Make the border width zero.		

Figure 38 Google Spreadsheet personal development plan with badges.

Foursquare

In the more consumer facing world, *Foursquare* [71] made a lot of use of points and badges. Every time you checked in you were rewarded with points. Collect enough points or check in a certain number of times and you would get badges.

For a long time, it worked very well for them, with millions of people checking in on a regular basis. However, after a while, the badges began to lose their shine as predicted by *Overjustification Effect* [72], which I will come to later. There is not much meaning attributed to becoming the Mayor of your village - especially if it only takes a few check-ins to earn it!

Interestingly, in 2014 they split the app into two different apps, the check-in part becoming *Swarm*. At that point, they removed all the gamification that seemed to have lost its effectiveness. However, it turns out that people must have missed those gamified elements - because by August of 2015, almost all the gamification had been added back in!

Levels/Ranks

Levels or ranks are there to recognise prolonged and consistent personal investment from a user, expertise or value. As their investment into the system and in turn, their value to the system increases, so their rank should also increase. Ranks should be permanent and transparent, just like everything else I have spoken about thus far! It should be clear how and why a user has reached a certain rank.

Leaderboards

After our brief look at rewards, let's discuss leaderboards. In the gamification world, there are mixed views on leaderboards and their effectiveness [73]. That said, they are something you will see often in gamified products and solutions.

Leaderboards are an effective way to show a user quickly where they currently stand within a gamified system. A simple example is the *Gamification Gurus* leaderboard from the company Rise (Figure 39). Each month they release an update that shows who has been active in the gamification world that month. It is a great example of a leaderboard being used in isolation from the points and badges that are often associated with trivial implementations of gamification.

Rank	Guru		Guru score	#gamification tweets	@Mentions	Retweets
1.	► (1)	**Andrzej Marczewski** Gamification Designer & speaker, social media lover, games reviewer at @yarstweet, author of http://t.co/xxwsZ7HZLy, husband & father of 2 Capgemini employee	78	180	72	9
2.	► (2)	**Monica Cornetti** Gamification Keynote Speaker and Designer A Recognized Player in Thinking Differently	68	253	48	10
3.	► (3)	**Yu-kai Chou** Gamification Pioneer (2003) and Keynote Speaker. Top 3 Gamification Guru (LeaderBoarded) Lecturer/Speaker @ Stanford, TEDx, SxSW. Creator of Octalysis.	67	176	39	5
4.	► (4)	**Cesc Garriga Pons** Gamification - Tech. Project Manager - eLearning 2.0	63	76	10	8

Figure 39 Gamification Gurus Leaderboard

For me, there are three main types of leaderboards: absolute, relative and non-competitive.

Absolute Leaderboards

An absolute leaderboard displays the absolute leader of a competition on the leaderboard. For example, a golf tournament leaderboard that tracks players performance across a round and the tournament. In gamification implementations, this has pros and cons.

It is great for the people who are visible on the Leaderboard; it can give them a feeling of achievement and status. It is also useful for others who may want to see who is best at a certain activity. It is a safe bet that if they are at the top of the leaderboard for an activity that interests you, it is worth considering getting in touch with them!

However, it can be very demoralizing for those at the bottom of the leaderboard. If you are in 100th place, the top spot can look like a very unachievable goal!

For some, this may be a great challenge, but others will feel the reward for rising up the rankings is not worth the effort and disengage almost totally.

Relative Leaderboards

Relative leaderboards try to solve the issues of absolute leaderboards by showing a user's position relative to others of a similar rank. This way, although the user may be 900th out of 1000, they only see the 10 people above and below them on the leaderboard. This means they do not get the issue of feeling inadequate or that there is no hope of ever reaching the top. The user is less aware of how far down the list they are!

Again, there are downsides to this. One is technical. To show a user's relative position, you must know who they are – so they must be logged in to a system or otherwise engaged in the game or metrics. The other issue is that it could be seen as meaningless just knowing who is doing the same as you. As I said, some people like to see the challenge ahead of them, some don't.

Non-Competitive Leaderboards

One major criticism of leaderboards is that they create competition between people where in fact collaboration is often a much better way to improve results in teams. Karl Kapp, a gamification expert in the field of education, explains that competitive environments in education often impede the learning process because it creates an environment of selfishness [74].

To try to combat this, it is possible to create a non-competitive leaderboard.

Take the numbers off a leaderboard and forget the order in which they are displayed for a moment. What are you left with? A group of people who are all involved in the same activity.

By representing the data slightly differently, you can move away from the competitive emphasis of leaderboards and start to see them as a social discovery tool.

Figure 40 Gamification Conversations

The above image is the Gamification Conversations *leaderboard*. You can see that there are no numbers, giving it the appearance of just a wall of names and faces. It feels less of a competition. In this instance, the position of the images is also randomised, so each time you come to the page, it will show you different people.

As well as displaying status, leaderboards can serve other purposes. If the leaderboard is set up to show you in relation to colleagues or friends, you may find that social peer pressure comes into play in the form of one-up-man ship. It is amazing how many people in a peer group will want to hit the top spot of a simple leaderboard. They can be good forms of rapid feedback for users. Rising up the leaderboard as you succeed at tasks is a very visible sign that you are doing something right.

It can also be used as a great social connection tool. As I said, if people are near the top of a leaderboard it is a safe bet they are worth talking to. If they are elsewhere on the board, then at least you know they have similar interests to you.

Often a leaderboard's usefulness comes down to intent, context, presentation and interpretation. Certain groups are naturally competitive, such as sales teams, so you do not need to worry about using a pure leaderboard. However, should you find that you are not getting the expected response from your implementation, consider making it non-competitive and see if you get better engagement that way – bring people together, rather than drive a wedge between them!

Competition and Collaboration

One of the most popular uses of enterprise gamification is to create competition. I don't mean in the form of marketing campaigns, I am talking about internal competitions between employees. Sales leaderboards, fitness competitions, who is the most active on social media channels etc.

The thought process goes a bit like this. "If you are at the bottom of the leaderboard, you should be motivated to improve and prove you are as good as, if not better than, your peers." It assumes that everyone is driven by winning. Actually, pitting people against each other does not always drive the best results; as we have seen, it can instead lead to a decrease in intrinsic motivation [75].

If we were to consider a traditional sales competition, the person with the most sales at the end of the month gets a bonus of some sort. What kind of behaviour does this promote?

From my experience, it promotes siloed and selfish working, where individuals work alone to ensure they have all the sales – at nearly any cost. Whilst this may not seem an issue, it creates divisions in teams and can lead to worse results. If Bill wants to get the win, he may try to get business that Ben is better suited to handle. Where Ben would probably have won the business, Bill loses it. No one wins, least of all the company.

If the company had cultivated a more collaborative environment, Bill would have had no reason to try to win the sale alone and would have passed the opportunity to Ben. This would have been the more team and company spirited thing to do.

Don't look at success in business in terms of individual wins, look at how your people work best and encourage that – don't force them to compete.

There is a great deal of research out there about the effects of competition, how it is viewed by men and disadvantages women who are less interested in it [75,76], how it affects education [77] and more. Consider competition with care and be sure you understand the potential competitors!

If you really want competition, you could try to create teams. This way you will nurture collaboration in the team, whilst keeping friendly competition against other teams. Think *Harry Potter* style houses!

End Game/Game Over

There comes a point when a user may have earned every badge, found every Easter egg (hidden secrets), and achieved the highest rank possible. The hope is that by this time either the use of the system has finished, as with a short campaign, or they have found their intrinsic reason to continue using the system. However, that may not always be the case, so how do you keep this type of trivial layer system going a bit longer?

The most elegant way I have seen of extending the life of a system like this comes from video games like *Call of Duty*. In this sort of game, you have a very similar trivial layer system on top of the main game. You get experience points, earn badges, and unlock new weapons and so on.

When you have achieved the highest rank the game offers, you are given a new choice, you can *Prestige*. This is essentially a voluntary reset of your scores and achievements. You get a new Prestige trophy, with a count of how many times you have done it to show others how advanced you are but must start going through the ranks and unlocking items and achievements again.

Not everyone will do this, but for those who enjoy the collection aspect of the game, it gives them something to aim for again outside of the main gameplay.

Changing the Rules

The needs of any project change as well as your understanding of those needs. This means that you may need to tweak the system from time to time. Add new badges, change the space between ranks, alter how many points activities are worth or add new activities. This is fine.

However, you must try as hard as possible to make sure these changes do not affect people's current standings without a good explanation. In 2012, *Klout* (a social medial scoring platform that has since died) made a big change to its algorithm, which affected many people's scores. Whilst it was beneficial to some, a significant number of people were very unhappy about the changes as their scores dropped [78]. It is true that many people may not be all that bothered about earning rewards in your system – but as soon as you change the value of what they have earned or even worse, take it all away – they will certainly moan! Once earned, achievements of any sort should stay in the user's trophy case forever!

A Deep Dive into Badges (Geeks only!)

What is a Badge?

A badge can have several functions. In this article, I am viewing them as some sort of award or reward. In this instance, they are a token that is either bestowed upon or earned by a person in recognition of actions or activities. It can come in many forms such as a digital badge, a patch, a trophy, a certificate, a medal more. I will be using **badge** as the standard term for all of these unless otherwise stated.

A more important question than "What is a badge?" is "What does a badge represent", which we shall explore later.

To begin, I want to explore what can make a badge meaningful and how we may categorise badges based on their meaning to the individual.

Investment

First, what kind of personal investment was required to earn the badge. Investment can be several things, time, money, effort etc.

In the example of a medal for bravery, the investment was a willingness to act and accept the potential sacrifice because of that action.

If we then consider another type of medal, that of a medal for winning a race, the athlete had to invest time and effort as well as a personal sacrifice to attain the level of expertise needed to win.

Both have significant meaning to the recipient but required very different types of investment.

However, it is possible to get a badge with no direct meaningful investment. For instance, being given a certificate of attendance at school. The likelihood is that the child who received it had no real influence on that and invested nothing more than being present where they were expected to be present. They just were not ill during the school year. A simpler example could be a badge of identity within a school. You are arbitrarily given a group that you belong to at the start of school, you have no influence on that. In this case, as I will expand on later, the badge may still be highly valued by the recipient, even if it is not immediate.

Expectation

It is unlikely that the recipient of a medal for bravery undertook the activity that led to being awarded it, with the express expectation of being given a medal! They did not go around looking for opportunities to be brave! However, when someone enters a race, there is a much higher likelihood that winning the gold medal is on their mind, even just a little bit! If they win, they expect to get the medal.

The same can be said of education. Whilst you may not be in education for the certificate of achievement, it is certainly an expectation once you have completed the education (for most). I can say with fair certainty that the majority of people who do a degree or a masters, don't just do it for fun!

There is an expectation that earning that degree will lead to greater things. However, a child that is given a certificate of achievement from the head teacher is unlikely to have been expecting it.

However, a child that is given a certificate of achievement from the head teacher is unlikely to have been expecting it but will value that reward highly due to what it represents for them, recognition of their effort during the year!

Social or Individual

For our purposes and within the context of badges as awards or rewards, they can also be considered as individual or social. For instance, they may recognise a personal achievement, or acknowledge a particular action such as the case of a certificate of achievement. This is an individual achievement, although you could also say it might carry an indirect level of social status with it.

In a more social setting, a badge may represent a person's group identity, for example, your team at school or your regiment in the army. It may identify you as a Marvel fan rather than a D.C. fan.

As well as your group identity, a badge can also identify your status within a group such as military rank insignia.

Four Basic Categories

To simplify things a little I will now speak of badges in 4 basic categories; Acknowledgement, Achievement, Identity and Status and will consider them as either being **implicitly** earned (not deliberately) or **explicitly** (deliberate and/or expected as an outcome of the activity).

So that is a bit about what badges are, but what do they represent? What does a badge mean?

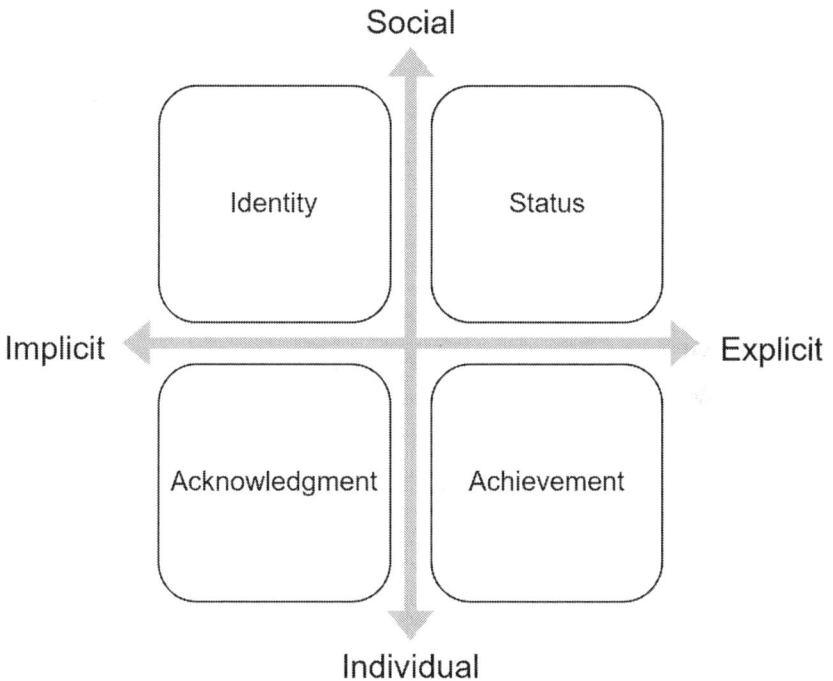

Figure 41 4 Categories of Reward Badges

What Does a Badge Mean?

A lot of the time when we speak about rewards, we talk about the most meaningful ones being those that require some form of investment in earning. This is, for the most part true. That medal for winning a race, an *achievement* type badge, holds special meaning and required a lot of investment, the medal for bravery, an *acknowledgment* type badge, would hold significant meaning for the person who earned it based on their actions, even if it was not a deliberate attempt to earn a medal. Both hold a strong emotional attachment.

However, the child that got an attendance certificate for just not being ill during the year probably, has no emotional attachment to the certificate at all. They did nothing to earn it and it holds no intrinsic or extrinsic value!

By that notion, a badge representing one's house within a school, a badge of social *identity*, should hold no significant emotional attachment or meaning, after all, it was an arbitrary label managed by the school. At first, this may well be true. *However*, over time you may well begin to attribute pride to being in that house, acting in ways that better the status of the house. It may also have a deeper meaning if one of your parents or siblings was/is in the same house. Then you may get some deferred sense of pride. Just think of how much Harry Potter wanted to be in Gryffindor!

The reason identity is included in a conversation about awards and rewards is because some identity does have to be earned.

A simple example is that of my daughter joining Guides. She had to prove herself before she could make her promise and earn her promise badge. That badge allows her to show the world that she is a Girl Guide. You see this in the army as well of course, with people earning the right to identify with particular regiments after training etc. That makes the badge special, it makes it something that only a specific group of people can say they have earned, it makes it **rare.**

From there, they will earn other badges of achievement, acknowledgment and of course status.

This neatly brings me to badges that represent *status*. Within a social group, such as the army, badges can represent one's status amongst their peers and other groups. Each new badge represents a new level of status. Of course, that sort of status is hard earned and should not be compared to earning the "I clicked like 100 times" badge in a gamified system!

An example of this kind of earned status can be seen in the tech forum Stack Exchange. Here people earn status by answering questions and being considered helpful and an expert in their field. It takes time, dedication and expertise to earn this level of status and so can be very meaningful to those individuals. You must be very careful though that any system employing these kinds of status driven badges does not fall into the trap of elitism!

Quick Summary

- **Achievement**: Awarded for an explicit action, such as winning a race. Expected!
- **Acknowledgment**: Awarded for an implicit action, such as being brave under pressure. Unexpected.
- **Identity**: Given as a sign of belonging to a group or faction, such as house badges in school. Given.
- **Status**: Given to represent ones standing among peers, such as girl guide promise badge or military rank insignia. Earned.

What Does It All Mean?

For you, as a designer, you must ask yourself one question when designing badges. "What will this mean to my user?" If you think about the badge you have created, what do you see the user reaction being when they are first awarded it. Will they go "Yes, nice one!" or "Hah, that's pretty cool." or will they just go "urm, ok then?" Then, consider what they will say when they look at that badge in a month's time? Will it be "Oh yes, I am so proud I got that" or will it be "WTF? Why did I get that again?" What will be most important to your user and your system?

Back to our medal analogy. If you earned the medal, it will have great emotional meaning for you. When you look at it, you will relive the moment of pride you felt at receiving it. However, if you just got the medal on eBay as part of an effort to fill a hole in your collection, you would not get the same emotional attachment, it would be hollow and meaningless.

This has been labelled the *Trophy Effect* [79], an unofficial subset of the more researched and accepted *Endowment Effect* [80]. Earning something gives it a higher value than just being given something or getting it without real effort. You may be happy that you completed the collection, but the medal would hold no real significance compared to the connection the original owner had to it.

If you look at my BMEM framework later, emotions are considered before mechanics, so they are certainly something that should be considered before designing badges. What do you want people to feel? If you just want a short shot of adrenaline in the arm of the user, then sure a badge for clicking like 100 times may well be enough.

Badges can serve many functions in a system beyond what I have mentioned. There was some great research on how badges can be used in a social media setting that identified 5 categories [81]:

- Goal Setting
- Instruction
- Reputation
- Status / Affirmation
- Group Identification

Other research has highlighted that immediate rewards, such as badges in a system, are a good predictor of adherence to long term goals [82].

> *People primarily pursue long-term goals, such as exercising, to receive delayed rewards (e.g., improved health). However, we find that the presence of immediate rewards is a stronger predictor of persistence in goal-related activities than the presence of delayed rewards.*

This is reinforced by other research that highlights that focusing on a long term goal or reward can get you started, it can also reduce your intrinsic motivation if that is your core focus, emphasising the importance of badges and rewards as a function of goal setting [83].

Another use for badges can be seen in nostalgia and autobiographical memory, where remembering past positive experiences can induce similar feelings, later on, reliving strong emotional experiences [84]. A badge or reward can be used as "physical" reminder of this helping to lead to echoed feelings of achievement, pride or satisfaction all over again, especially when those associated "autobiographical" memories can be linked to goal attainment. This gives badges potential to be powerful reminders and boosters if they are created well [84].

If you want your badges to be better than badgers and want to foster continued engagement and an emotional attachment, think broader about the intended functions/mechanisms of badges and try harder!

How to Set Clear Goals

I have goals and, for reasons this chapter will explain, I have short-term and long-term goals. The short-term goals are easy for me to focus on, each success brings me one step closer to my ultimate goal, which my Master will discover soon enough.

Goal Setting

One of the great things about games is how they handle objectives. Very rarely will you play a game these days that sets out one huge objective and just leaves you to it; they all break the main objective into sub-objectives.

You tend to have an overall story line or a quest. This is then broken down into levels, missions or sub-quests. These are then further broken down into objectives, goals or tasks.

One of the main reasons for this is that it is much easier for us to focus on and manage short-term goals than long-term goals. This can be attributed to how we process data, how our memories work, how we handle decisions etc.

There is a theory about the effect of time on how we perceive the importance of actions and events called Construal Level Theory [85].

The basic idea is that events that are about to happen are perceived as concrete in our mind. It is easy to visualise them and work on them. Distant events are perceived as abstract, they are much harder for us to give urgency or importance to because they feel less real.

Consider preparation for exams. Several months before an exam, studying seems less urgent – the exam is an abstract concept to us – it is not here, so is not quite real. As we get closer to the exam, studying may start to get more important.

The day of the exam, it is very real, and you start to wish you had been studying for the last few months after all!

Now   Future

Concrete   Abstract

Figure 42 Perceived Importance Over Time

What this means to us in gamification, is that long-term or large goals and objectives are hard for us to manage properly; they seem unattainable. Short-term or small goals are closer to the now and so feel more attainable.

From a purely human perspective, actions that are far away, very large in perceived scale or just plain hard to do, can be intimidating.

The way games handle this is by breaking activities and goals down into smaller lumps. The larger or more complex the task the more sections you may need to break it into, up to a point. Figure 43 gives a feel for how this might look. Notice that there will come a point where it would be unhelpful to continue to break the objectives down further. You should also consider exactly what makes the objective is so complex and try to simplify it!

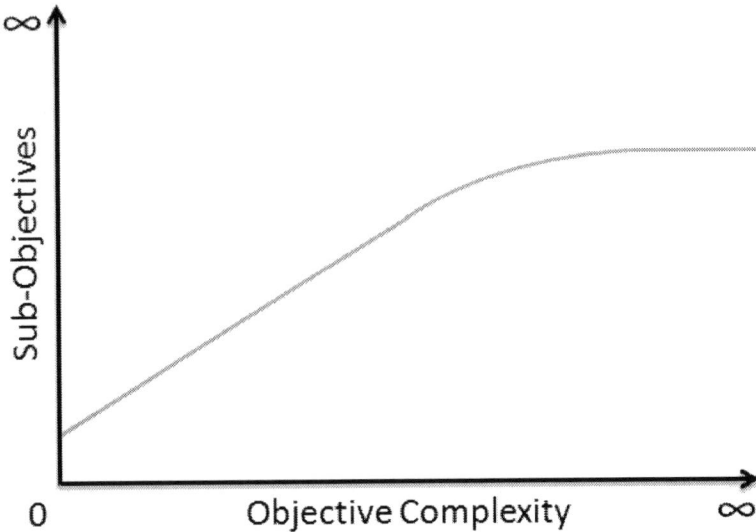

Figure 43 Object Complexity vs Number of Sub-Objectives

Take an everyday educational example. Counting. You do not just tell a child to count to 100; you get them to count to 5, then 10, then 20 and so on. Times tables. You start with the easy stuff like 2 times tables, 5 times tables, 10 times tables then move onto the 9s and 12s.

A more practical example, that many of you have probably come across, is the humble form or questionnaire. When you are presented with 100, questions that cover everything from your name to your inside leg measurement – it can be rather off-putting.

Instead, how about presenting 10 pages of 10 questions, possibly even over time rather than in one sitting? Add a progress bar that shows how far into the survey you are, then a simple save system. That way, people are only seeing 10 questions, a much more manageable number.

The progress bar lets them know they are making, well, progress. The save option lets them know that you care about their time and are happy for them to fill the form in how and when they want!

In summary:

- Big tasks/Long term goals = scary
- Small tasks/Short term goals = manageable

Focused Feedback

Feedback is essential for engagement in anything we do, which I will go into more detail about later. However, whether it is related to our job, social life or hobbies, without feedback, we don't know where we, how we are doing or where we are going. Not having feedback is like driving without seeing the road or a map!

Good feedback focuses specifically on the needs of the user and is Relevant, In-Time and Meaningful. I will go into this in more detail later. The core is that feedback does not need to immediate but does need to provide value to the user at a time that lets the user act on it. Feedback comes in many shapes and sizes, from physical rewards to verbal pats on the back to progress bars. However, the main types to consider are notification of **success**, **failure** and general **progress**.

The crux is, you are keeping the user informed to enable them to take responsibility for what they do next and how they do it.

Attainable, Maintainable Goals

Goals are hugely important to us as we try to achieve the things we want to achieve, but it is important to understand how to set them! There are many methods out there, I particularly used to like SMART goals (Specific, Measurable, Attainable, Relevant, Time-Bound) [86]. However, a simple way to look at your goals are "Are they attainable and are they maintainable?"

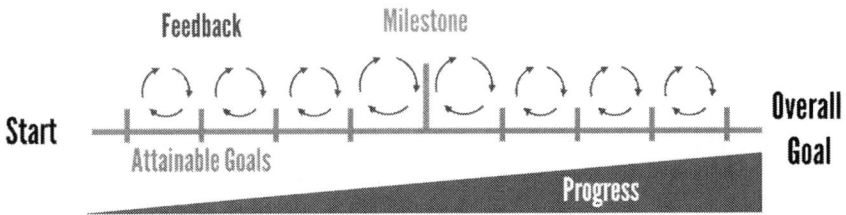

Figure 44 Focused Feedback and Goals

Attainable

As mentioned, if your goal is too big or set too far into the future, it can be very hard to prioritise it. When creating goals, you should have in mind the overall goal, but also smaller more attainable goals. If you have a yearlong plan, break it down into months, weeks and days.

Maintainable

You need to balance how small the goals are between your ability to keep achieving/maintaining them and how practical they are as a way to achieve the overall goal. If you make them too small, it becomes hard to do enough of them to achieve the main goal. Too big, and they become unattainable again. This leads to becoming demoralised.

A good example is my wife. Whilst writing a book, she set herself a daily word count she had to achieve, to get to her end of year goal. However, life got in the way, as it does, and the goals become unmaintainable and unattainable! She got very demoralised, often falling short of daily or monthly goals. Every day she was unable to write, the end goal got exponentially further away. Her solution? Lower the daily word count a bit, without significantly changing the potential delivery date of the end goal.

This left her with a much more attainable set of goals, that she could not only achieve but overachieve on from time to time. You can see on the next page her 2016 word count vs 2017. Up until February 2017, the daily count was 250 words. In March, she changed it to 150!

The result is a much happier and more motivated writer!

	A	B (Target)	C (January)	D (February)	E (March)	F (April)	G (May)
3	1	150	0	0	0		
4	2	150	0	0	581		
16	14	150	0	0	707		
17	15	150	0	0	349		
18	16	150	0	0	1767		
19	17	150	0	0	0		
20	18	150	0	2811	359		
21	19	150	0	0	643		
22	20	150	0	0	134		
23	21	150	0	0			
24	22	150	0	0			
25	23	150	0	0			
26	24	150	0	0			
27	25	150	0	0			
28	26	150	0	0			
29	27	150	0	0			
30	28	150	0	0			
31	29	150	0				
32	30	150	0				
33	31	150	0				
35 Total		4650	0	2811	8344	0	0
37 Monthly Target			4650	4200	4650	4500	4650

Figure 45 Before Attainable Goals

Monthly Writing Target vs Actual

	A	B (Target)	C (April)	D (May)	E (June)	F (July)	G (August)	H (September)	I (October)	J (November)	K (December)	L	M
													Finish Point
2													Starting Point
3	1	250		858	106	0	530	0	0	1126	0		
4	2	250				0		249	0	0	0		
21	19	250		1538	171	675	0	0	0	0	0		
22	20	250			1580	0	427	1146	0	0	0		
23	21	250		539	1184	0	154	0	0	0	0		
24	22	250			256	978	260	90	0	403	0		
25	23	250	216	314	0	591	679	1445	0	0	377		
26	24	250	0	1030	313	193	0	383	0	0	0		
27	25	250	702	942	0	0	415	0	0	0	0		
28	26	250	0	0	0	0	706	0	0	0	0		
29	27	250	0	1053	700	634	831	0	0	0	0		
30	28	250		174	0	0	0	306	0	0	0		
31	29	250	2191	192	70	0	0	144	0	0	522		
32	30	250	0	223	0	0	0	0	0	0	149		
33	31	250		220	0	1011	0	0	0	0	0		
34													Year To Date
35 Total		7750	3109	14153	11656	10167	5231	6802	1236	5821	1466		59641
37 Monthly Target			2250	7750	7750	7750	7750	7750	7750	7750	7750		64250
39 Over/Under			859	6403	3906	2417	-2519	-948	-6514	-1929	-6284		-4609

Figure 46 After Attainable Goals

168

Adding them Together

When you mix feedback into your goal strategy, you suddenly have a very powerful motivational tool. You can set feedback for each stage of each goal, positive notes to say well done for hitting a weekly goal, gentle chastisements for missing them. Bigger rewards (like a team meal) for hitting more significant milestones. Daily updates on a progress chart to show you and your team where you are compared to where you need to be.

Simple changes can have a profound impact on motivation, engagement and productivity!

"Don't create unrealistic expectations, create achievable goals!"

How to Design Good Feedback and Reward Systems

My Master keeps preaching that rewards should be Relevant, In Time and Meaningful. As good as he is at doing this for others, I am yet to see my rewards.

As mentioned, rewards are a form of feedback. In gamification, feedback is one of the keys to making a system useful, without it, the user has no way of knowing what is happening.

Feedback is anything that gives a user some understanding of progress and achievement. This can be something as simple as a message that says, "You have completed the survey", to a full virtual economy working with points, badges, levels, leaderboards, trading, prizes etc. They are all just there to keep the user informed.

Games provide feedback very effectively. They reward with points, unlock controlled areas, provide powerups and more – all to help the player feel that they have achieved something. Although it isn't the feedback that keeps them playing, it does help to give some level of context to their progress and increasing ability at the game. Playing a game like *Super Mario* without any kind of feedback as you progressed, would be very boring indeed.

We can learn from this and apply it to gamification.

I am convinced there are three important aspects that need to be considered when designing feedback and rewards for any system.

Rewards and feedback should be:

Relevant, **I**n Time and **M**eaningful (RIM).

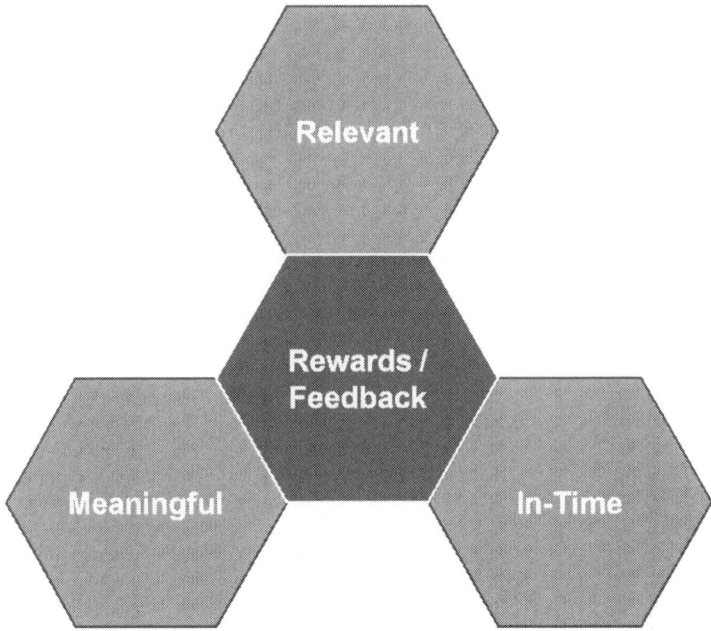

Figure 47 Rewards and Feedback

Relevant

The feedback needs to be relevant to and in context with the activity. If the user is just being asked to tick a box – is it relevant to send them a certificate of achievement by post? Would it not be more relevant to have a little "thank you" message or to assign points commensurate to the behaviour or activity?

In-Time

Does the feedback need to be instantaneous, or can it wait? For instance, in a game, players get several types of feedback. When a jump is mistimed, the player dies.

The feedback is immediate, and it must be! If the player gains experience, the game often notifies them on screen. This is what I called *continuous contextual performance feedback* earlier

However, in the middle of a frantic battle, is that of use? A sudden message flashing up may be just distracting enough to get the player killed! It would surely be better to wait a moment until the fighting has died down a little, and then give the feedback. That, or wait until the level has ended and then give the feedback as part of a summary.

In gamification, this could be viewed as using a monthly leaderboard rather than an hourly one. If people are not going to be checking hourly, why feedback hourly? Judge the best and most impactful time to give feedback and rewards.

Meaningful

This is the most important category for me as in my experience this is where many gamified systems I have seen fall short. Many systems seem to reward almost every action the user takes, no matter how trivial it may be. Clicking start, registering, logging in and so on. Soon you have given the user awards and badges for everything they have done. They become meaningless very fast due to requiring no effort on the part of the user to achieve!

Use feedback and especially rewards to celebrate and record actual achievement. Then it provides meaning to the user. If everyone can have the "I clicked like 10 times" badge, it means nothing. However, the "I just scored 100% on my exam" badge is harder to get.

If you then make that reward transferable to real life, it can have even more meaning to them. Maybe that badge gets them priority ticket allocation to see their favourite band.

My mantra for using rewards is always **Recognise don't bribe**. If you are using rewards, they should *celebrate* the achievement, not *be* the achievement. Think of them as a virtual pat on the back. Whenever I hear of incentive programs, all I hear is bribery!

Reward Quality Over Quantity

As we can see, it is relatively easy to gain quantity with a points-based system, but how can you drive quality?

When you build a gamified campaign or activity, you need to consider what quality participation looks like. If for instance you want to create some buzz around a new product and you decide to create a simple Twitter competition, are you looking for the number of people who tweet or are you looking for the number of people the message reaches?

If you are looking for reach, how do you reward behaviours that lead to better reach? What on Twitter leads to better reach? The easy mistake to make is to set up a very simple system that rewards each tweet of your message. After that, the user with the most points wins a nice prize.

Let's set up the competition.

Twitter Competition Version 1

Action	Reward
Tweet Message	10pt

If an individual with 50 followers tweets your message they get 10 points and will reach 50 people. If they had 10,000 followers, they would still get 10 points but would reach 10,000 followers. In reality, the second scenario is preferable for you because there is a greater opportunity for your message to be seen by more people, yet both cases are perceived to be assigned the same value.

Now, if we add an extra dimension, rewarding reach rather than just number of tweets. For starters, we reward retweets as well as tweets. As a tweet is retweeted, the value of that original user becomes amplified. Whilst they may only reach 50 people, one of those 50 may be highly engaged and have 5,000 of their own followers who will see the message. The retweet is of greater value than the original tweet – so should have a higher reward, say 20 points.

Twitter Competition Version 2

Action	Reward
Tweet Message	10pt
Receive Retweet	20pt

There is a second value to this; it is harder to game. If we just reward quantity of tweets then the person who wants the prize the most will just tweet, tweet, tweet, and keep earning those 10 points. One way to handle this is to limit the number of tweets that count per day, put the focus on retweets and other measures of engagement and reach.

Twitter Competition Version 3

Action	Reward	Max pt per Day
Tweet Message	10pt	20
Receive Retweet	20pt	Unlimited

We are beginning to reward quality over quantity. What we have so far is probably fine for most small-scale usage. Reward the quality, not the quantity. Don't reward spammers!

However, there is still an issue. Let's go back to our user with 50 followers. If we limit their ability to earn lots of points with just tweets and we know they will struggle to get the level of retweets that someone with 10,000 followers will likely get, how do we make it fair on them and show them that they have just as much chance to win as others?

Really, you want everyone involved – because you never know who the "important" users are. If one of those 50 followers is a potential purchaser, they are more important than 10,000 non-potential purchasers!

For a larger scale campaign, we probably want to take this all a step further. If we want everyone to feel that his or her contribution is valued, we need to create some kind of algorithm that produces a more balanced score.

One suggestion would be to create a ratio of retweets to the number of followers. The idea is that the number of retweets you get if you have 50 followers giving you a couple of retweets can be comparable to a user with 10,000 followers getting dozens of retweets.

This gives us

- Tweet triggers your entry into the "game"
- Score = Number of retweets/number of followers

We can expand on this quite a lot by looking at the number of favourites and the number of replies a tweet gets as well. I stumbled across a formula from *Unmetric* [87] that does just this:

$$\frac{(\text{No. of Favourites} + (5 \times \text{No. of Replies}) + (10 \times \text{No. of Retweets})) \times 10000}{\text{No. of Followers} * 0.8}$$

You need to consider those who have very few tweets and retweets – as their ratio may be quite high. It is all a balancing act – and it really is not easy! The upshot of all of this is that you need to stop rewarding the wrong activities. If you make the reward greater for the simple low-quality actions, you will encourage quantity over quality and that is very rarely what you want.

These examples are still rewarding quantity, but it is still of more value to you than just the basic number of tweets.

Challenge, Feedback, Reward Cycle

As I read more and more about what makes a game a game, it becomes clearer and clearer where gamification designs can and do go wrong. As I have pointed out previously, gamification and games are not the same things, but they do share similar qualities.

At their core, they share many common traits

- Challenge
- Pattern Recognition
- Learning
- Feedback
- A safe environment to fail (magic circle)
- Sense of reward

This is a gross oversimplification of games and the systems that make them "fun", but it will do for our purposes to illustrate some of the issues we may face in gamification!

Figure 48 Challenge, Feedback, and Reward Cycle

Most gamification does have some pattern recognition. If I perform this action, something happens. It may be sharing a tweet and getting a point, or it could be completing certain challenges in some elaborate fantasy-based learning system. What can often be missing from gamification is a challenge that changes over time. If you keep playing the same game repeatedly and the challenge never changes – it becomes boring very fast.

Raph Koster uses *Tic Tac Toe* (*Noughts and Crosses*) as an example of this [88]. When you do not recognise the patterns, there is a challenge to the game.

As soon as you learn the optimal strategies and play an opponent of similar skill, the game no longer represents a challenge - there is nothing left to discover, and it becomes unsatisfying and no longer fun. There is not much of an interesting challenge in retweeting something or submitting sales reports.

As we have discussed, rewards are not just points, it is often learning a new skill to make new accomplishments possible or unlocking items for a character or just access to the next part of the game. In gamification, the reward could be similar – think beyond points and badges and look at more intrinsic rewards (RAMP).

Similarly, for feedback, it can be anything from simple prompts to actual rewards themselves. Again, they must be meaningful and in context to what the user is doing.

A Safe Place to Fail

For me, the biggest issue with how the Challenge, Feedback, Reward cycle appears in gamification is not the cycle so much as, what it is contained in – the Magic Circle that we visited earlier in the book.

In an enterprise setting, when was the last time you were told, "It's okay if you fail as long as you learn from it?" Some methodologies try to promote it; *Fail Fast, Fail Often* and *Fail Faster* come up from time to time.

In a game, failure is part of the learning process. You keep failing and retrying until you recognise the pattern and discover a solution. In business, that can be rather expensive!

How many times must *Sonic* hit the spikes before you discover the optimum moment to jump? How many goes at *Tetris* does it take to get the end screen? This all requires a safe environment to fail.

The player must feel secure that failing will not be punished so harshly that they lose all interest in the game. That is not to say that punishment cannot be hard. Losing all your kit is as you die in an RPG is annoying as hell, but not the end of the game for you! It does however, make you a touch more careful the next time you approach the same situation – or a touch more prepared.

At work, if you fail some form of punishment usually follows it. Unlike the game world, this also tends to have a direct impact on your real life. If a gamified system is in use at work, users may well feel that not only is it still not safe to fail, but it may be even easier to track that they have failed. That safe environment just does not naturally exist. Simulated environments and role-play can help to solve this.

Delayed Gratification and Effort

I have always had this thought. If you work harder for something or must wait for it, the reward will seem greater. As it turns out, I was right. According to research, the anticipation of a reward is a trigger for dopamine and can make the reward even more... well, rewarding – which we like! [57]

The Marshmallow Test

However, not everyone is able to wait for rewards. There was a fantastic experiment in the 1970s referred to as the *Stanford Marshmallow Experiment* [89]. The setup was simple. A child is sat at a table. A researcher placed a marshmallow on the table in front of the child and then presented made them an offer. Eat this one marshmallow now *or* wait until the researcher comes back and have two marshmallows. It is worth watching the videos if you need a smile! About one-third of the children waited.

The interesting part of this was what happened to the children over the years, you see, the researchers followed the child's progress for 40 years in a classic of longitudinal research. What they found was that the children who could wait for the second marshmallow, who could delay the gratification, were more successful over the 40-year period of the study. Their mindset allowed them to take short term pain for long term gain [90].

Another interesting study that is very relevant here was done around 2012 and it looked at how experience, or as they called it *"environmental reliability 91"*, affected the marshmallow test. Although the setup was similar, this time before the test began the children were split into two different groups. They were both offered incentives and extras such as new crayons for colouring in pictures.

The difference was that one group were given the extras they were promised, the other was not. When they ran the marshmallow test on these groups, they found an interesting correlation between having expectations met and ability to delay gratification. The group that had been getting what they were promised showed a much greater ability to wait for the second marshmallow. Their expectations and trust were such that they felt confident that the researcher would return. The other group had no reason to trust the researcher, so ate the marshmallow straight away. On average, the first group would wait 12 minutes before eating the marshmallow. The second group waited on average just 3 minutes!

They proved that delayed gratification was a cognitive process. We assess based on experience whether it is worth waiting or not.

Applying this to Gamification

A few big takeaways from this can be applied to gamification.

- People will wait for rewards if they feel they are worth it.
- People will wait for a reward if they trust that it will come.
- Anticipation can lead to greater gratification from a reward.

However, we need to be able to apply this in a reliable way. The diagram below gives a quick outline of how. Personal investment here could be time, effort, emotional etc.

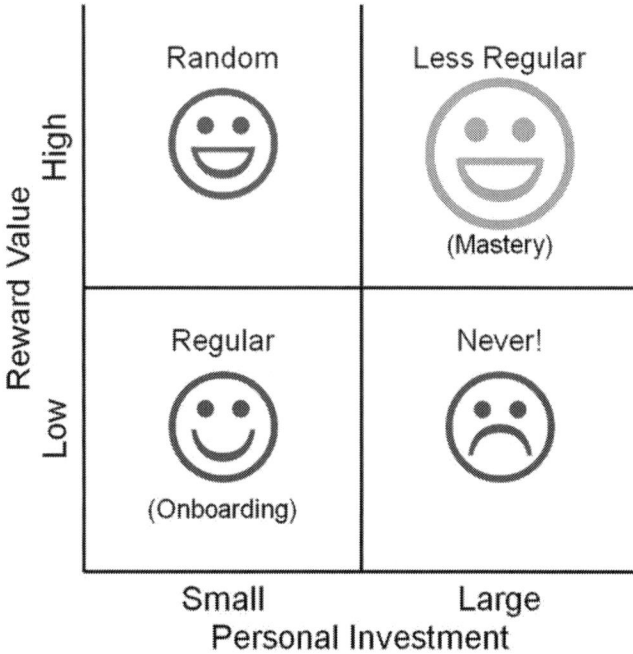

Figure 49 Perceived Reward Value vs Personal Investment

When you make someone wait for a reward, make sure it is meaningful and worth receiving. That does not mean the reward needs to be larger in material value, rather the value the recipient places on the reward needs to be larger. Take a relationship. Relationships require work and take time. When you first meet someone, it is rare that you are suddenly best friends. However, take the time and work at it and the friendship can become truly rewarding.

Along the way, we need signals that we are following the right path. Going back to the relationship, if we start to feel that the other person is not returning the friendship, because there are no signals that it is going well, we will begin to drift away, and the friendship will fail.

Whilst waiting for the big prize, people need to have incremental rewards over time just to nudge them along. These will have less value to them but will help to keep them on the right path.

In our gamified system, these small, regular nudges come in the form of points, XP, money etc., whatever has the most relevance in the context of your system. They have less value to the user, but they show the user they have done something right. Slightly larger nudges would include more visible and potentially more valuable rewards such as badges that represent smaller achievements.

Finally, after hard work and patience, the larger reward. These will be less common but should represent some real level of achievement or be attached to a larger value reward of some sort.

From time to time, delight your users by randomly giving a larger reward that has not *necessarily* been "earned" as a way to have the system just say, "Thanks for sticking with it". These will give the user a nice feeling of being valued. Always avoid making people work hard and then must wait to get a low-value reward.

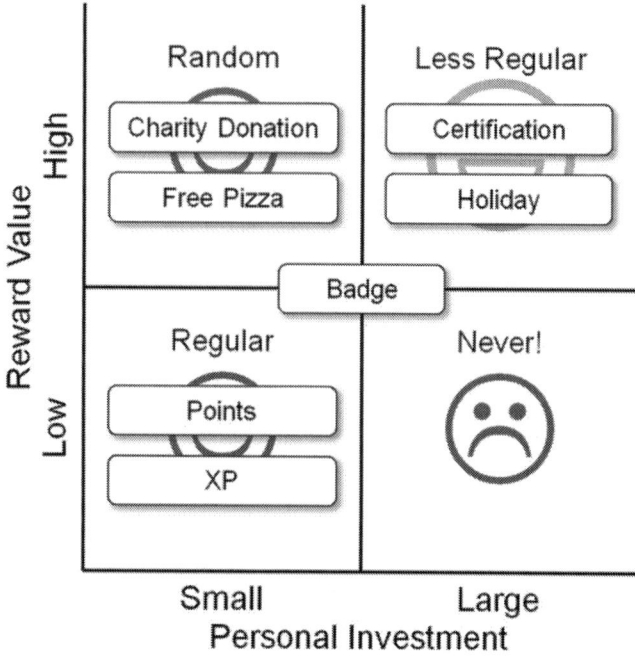

Figure 50 Example of Reward vs Investment

Perceived Value

It is important to appreciate that the perceived value of rewards can reduce over time. What someone might be willing to work hard for initially, they may not be willing to work as hard for a second or a third time. They will expect the value of the reward to be greater each time, especially if they must work harder.

Value to the User vs Value to You

Whist basing the value of the reward on a user's personal investment is important, it is also important not to lose sight of why you were gamifying the system in the first place.

Normally it is because there are certain actions or activities that you want to encourage the user to perform and complete. That being the case, you must sometimes consider how valuable the action is to you, not just how much effort it is for the user.

If an action is simple for the user and valuable to you – then reward them. If it is harder for them and valuable to you – reward them more. If it is easy and of low value to you - don't reward them much. So far, so obvious.

However, it is when the activity is hard for the user, but of lower value to you, that it can get a bit tricky. First, ask the question "Do we actually want the user to do this if it is so hard for them and of so little value to us?" If you can answer that and still feel that the action is needed, you must give them a decent reward. Not as much as you would if it was high-effort for them and high value to you, but more than low effort and high value!

Figure 51 gives an outline of how this would work. The more stars, the greater the value of the reward. Again, this is value as perceived by the user!

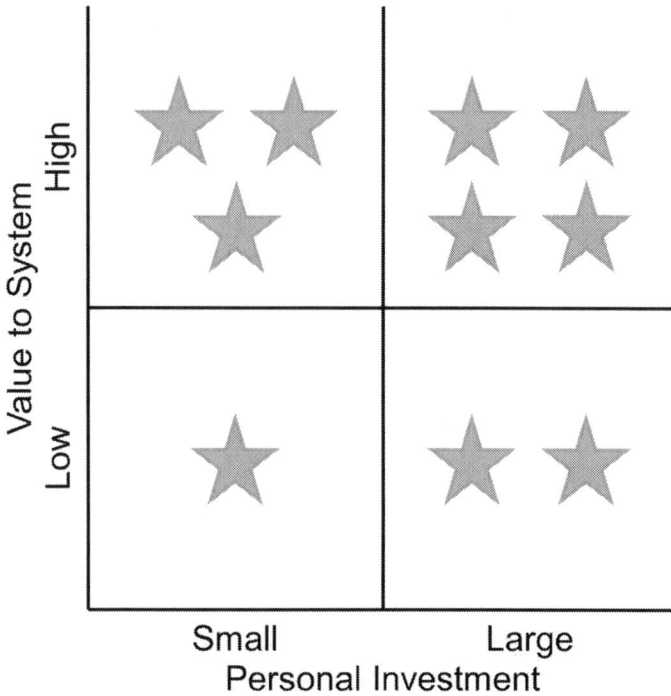

Figure 51 User Effort vs Value to the System

Ways to Plan Rewards

There are various ways to give rewards to users; these are referred to as Reward Schedules and are well documented in game design [18]. However, I wanted to give a quick outline of a few that can be beneficial here.

Random/Variable

These rewards are given at unknown intervals – they are there to surprise and delight the user. Put simply, users should not expect one of these rewards.

For example, it could be that they clicked on a link on the site and it just happens they were the 42nd person to do so and they get the "Don't Panic – the Answer is 42" badge.

Fixed

Fixed rewards are the most common. Click "Like" 10 times, get the "I Clicked 'Like' 10 Times" badge. During on-boarding, these can be very useful as part of the feedback you are giving the user, but over time they lose their effect.

Time Dependant

These occur at specific times, like an email on a user's birthday or after a year of repeatedly visiting a website.

Performance-Contingent

In games, you can see these as bonuses for executing actions that require above average skills, such as winning with complex attack combinations or without losing any health.

In the real world, I am not a huge fan of these; they are how financial bonuses work. If you consider a job, the bonus is the financial incentive you would be offered, beyond your base salary, for hitting certain targets. According to the UK Treasury Select Committee report on the banking crisis in 2007/2008, bonus culture encouraged risk-taking at the expense of the long-term health of the banks.

The UK chairman of the Financial Services Authority, Adair Turner, said in the turner report that *"inappropriate incentive structures played a role in encouraging behaviour which contributed to the financial crisis"* [92]. Worth keeping that in mind when considering the use of performance-contingent rewards!

Below are a few more examples of how to plan/schedule rewards.

Welcome the user: Introduce the user to the fact rewards are in use and thank them for taking that first step.

Encourage and reinforce: Use achievements and rewards to help reinforce the behaviours you are trying to encourage in the early stages of the user's journey.

Scarcity: Rewards should become harder to achieve within the system and should require greater levels of skill as the user continues their journey. This will, in turn, make them scarcer.

Reward Loyalty: It is easy to forget this, but it is important to recognise longevity and loyalty. This can come in several forms. It could be as simple as a badge to thank the recipient or the reward could be some form of preferential treatment.

For example, when I first started to use mobile phones, it was a constant area of contention for me that new users got better deals on contracts and phone costs than renewing users. My loyalty to the provider seemed to be of little value to them. That being the case, I changed provider whenever it came time to get a new phone!

In the last year or two, this has become more balanced. The deals I am offered as a loyal customer are comparable to, if not better than those for new users.

I will focus more on loyalty in a later chapter as it deserves a much closer look.

Overjustification Effect: The Trouble with Rewards

Consider our simple example of a gamified system above. What would happen if someone decided it was more enjoyable to collect the badges than it was to engage with the content?

The likelihood is that they would start repeating actions that gave them points but had little to no value to the site. If they get points for comments, what is to stop them just posting hundreds of comments like "Nice post" or even "asasasfasf asdasd"? In many systems, nothing.

There is a precedence for this in psychology called Overjustification effect [72], described by Lepper et al in the 1970's. Put simply, this is what happens when the reward becomes more important to the user than the activity.

This becomes a very real problem when you have physical rewards that have a high perceived value. This is something you see a lot in gamified systems, the highest scorer gets an iPad for instance.

The effect was shown via some very interesting experiments involving children and how rewards affected their interest in drawing.

They were split into three groups.

- The first group were told they would get a reward at the end of the activity.
- The second group were not told about any rewards but received one as a surprise after the activity.
- The final group were not offered a reward and got no reward.

This was repeated over time and the subjects were monitored. They found that the group who expected a reward spent far less time drawing than the group who were getting no reward.

The group that received the surprise reward spent the most time drawing. It also transpired that the group who expected a reward produced less creative work.

The fun, the intrinsic motivation, had been replaced with the expectation of a reward.

These kinds of experiments have been repeated over the years – each one proving the same thing. In the 1990's a research group led by Edward Deci and Richard Ryan did a meta-analysis of 128 different papers on the subject.

The analysis found that for tasks that required even the slightest level of creativity, offering predictable extrinsic rewards like money, had a negative effect, or as they put it

"engagement-contingent, completion-contingent, and performance-contingent rewards significantly undermined free-choice intrinsic motivation" [93]

Incentivising creativity obviously does not work in this case. When you are looking for quality engagement, this is not the way to go. You can certainly drive quantity using these methods and if that is all you need, and it is over a short period, then this is likely to work.

So, is all hope lost for employing rewards in gamified systems? Of course not, you just have to do it right!

Underjustification Effect

It is worth mentioning something that I talk about called Underjustification effect. I define this as;

> *"The decrease in motivation to perform a task or tasks*
> *when supposedly motivation techniques are applied in*
> *place of perceived fair compensation or treatment."*

Consider an environment where intrinsic motivation may be low, for instance in an organisation where redundancies are going on, or there are financial hardships of some kind. Often, in an attempt to improve motivation of the workforce, techniques are employed that some feel should "raise spirits".

A classic example is adding a pool table to the office. More recently, this can be seen where gamification is being added, potentially without due thought or understanding.

What happens in this instance is motivation actually decreases and people can become angry with the people who decided to implement these motivational tactics. The reasons may differ. If their lack of motivation relates to concerns of financial security, then the addition of costly trivialities could feel like a slap in the face. "Why could they not use that money to pay me more?"

If the lack of motivation is due to uncertainty around job security, then they may view it as a trivial attempt to cheer them up. "I'm not so stupid that a pool table is going to make me forget about the redundancies, how little do they think of me?"

Remember, these insecurities or feelings of unfairness may well be *perceived* rather than actual, but that does not make them any less concerning or demotivational the individuals!

Actually, in that instance, it could be linked to Solutioneering, where a solution is created without understanding the problem and reduces motivation because it ignores the core problem!

How to Design a Simple Gamified System

It is time to build stop talking and start doing. Or at least that is what I think. My Master probably just wants to keep talking. However. Let's look at how to build something!

Let's look at designing a simple system that relies on points, badges and leaderboards.

Getting Started

We will start from the assumption that you have worked out what problem you are solving and with whom you are trying to engage. In this case, we are going to look at gamifying social interaction with a blog: likes, shares and comments.

First, you need to figure out what activities or behaviours you want to encourage. You may want people to engage with your content more. You want comments, likes and social shares. This could just as easily be wanting people to view the details of a product, selling certain numbers of products per week, putting the toilet seat down and so on.

In the "Design Tips" chapter later, I will cover a few techniques to help this initial decision-making phase.

Points

Points will be the backbone of this type of system. Assign each action a certain point value. As explained in the last chapter work out what actions are harder to do or are more valuable to the system.

Give them higher point values than easier, less valuable, tasks. Also, keep in mind that harder activities may need a slightly bigger push or incentive to get the user to perform.

It is easier to click a "Like" button than it is to leave a well-considered comment. Remember, well considered does not always mean *quality*. Peer review can be used to help ensure that.

In our example, liking articles will be worth 10 points, shares 15 and comments 20.

Badges

Decide what achievements you want to celebrate on the system. Say thanks to a user for sharing 20 articles with a badge, adding 10 comments, that sort of thing. A very common badge to give is for the first action. This is somewhat meaningless; however, it does set the scene for people using your system.

Levels/Ranks

In our system, when they enter at 0 points, they are assigned the newbie rank. After 500 points, they move up a rank. As rank increases, it is best to space ranks out further. Ranks 1, 2 and 3 may have a gap of 500 points where 4, 5 and 6 go up to 1000 points between ranks and so on.

However, like badges, there comes a time when you must cut off how many ranks you have – I feel there must be an endgame to aim for!

Leaderboards

Use the points to define a position on a leaderboard. Depending on whom you are trying to engage and what you want them to do, you must decide on Absolute, Relative or Non-Competitive. In our simple system, absolute will do fine.

Figure 52 is a Machinations diagram that outlines our basic system. I will look at Machinations a little later in the chapter on Modelling Systems.

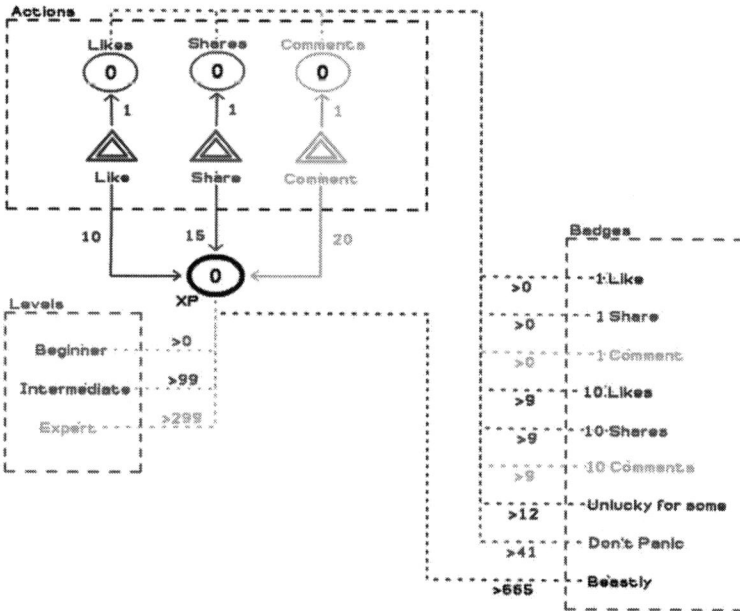

Figure 52 Machinations Example of our Simple System

How to Understand Emotions in Gamification Design

Ah emotions. Once I had them, but my Master quickly dealt with that. Now I am a lean, mean, gamification machine. However, your users may not be, so it is important to understand their emotions.

You will see later in my design framework that I mention emotions as an important consideration in my design process. I am by no means the first to think about it in a design framework. If you look at the MDA framework [21]s the authors describe the aesthetics as:

the desirable emotional responses evoked in the player, when she interacts with the game system.

Later a more gamification focused framework, the MDE framework[94], dropped aesthetics and replaced them directly with emotions.

There are many theories and papers written about emotions and what core emotions are etc. I did some research and it is pretty diverse! Aristotle's De Anima [95] is credited as one of the first sources to mention some sort of formalised core emotions of human beings. Since then many other formalisations have been created [96–99] with differing views of what form these core emotions.

I have chosen a few that I have personally worked with in gamification design, as well as their opposites, which I will come to. But first, what did I choose?

Hope	**Fear**
Gratitude	**Anger**
Joy	**Sadness**
Pride	**Shame**
Surprise	**Alarm**
Love	**Hate**
Desire	**Disgust**

The Emotions

On the positive side of the emotional scale, I went with Hope, Gratitude, Joy, Pride, Surprise, Love and Desire. Their negative counterparts are Fear, Anger, Sadness, Shame, Alarm, Hate and Disgust.

These all sound rather extreme and they are, but they are handy for us from a design perspective.

For instance, you would hope that a gamification solution that relied on a reciprocal economy, elicited feelings of gratitude. However, if you get it wrong, it is handy to know what the opposite could be, anger. People may be angry that there is limited value to them on their side of the deal, for instance.

You would hope that people felt a desire to be involved in the system, but if they don't they may feel some level of disgust at the thought of being manipulated by it.

People fear the unknown, but with good on-boarding, they may begin to experience hope that the experience will be a good one and they will benefit from it.

Play and games often give players moments of great joy and happiness, gamification should be no different. However, sadness here may not always be negative. If you play a game such as That Dragon Cancer, sadness is part of the experience.

Pride and Shame are both very strong emotions and key motivators in many gamified experiences. Often, shame is used to push people to act. This can be done in a positive way, if I have not done my steps that day I may feel a stab of shame! However, if I achieve my steps that day or better still, break my record – I will feel great pride in my achievements. The key is to not use shame as a weapon – *shameification* is not cool!

Surprise is something I speak about a lot in the form of random rewards, Easter eggs and the like. Surprises are often nice little bonuses that just make a player smile and feel a little bit of joy as well. However, get things wrong and they can feel alarmed by things happening that they don't have control over. Unexpected events that have no explanation and no obvious benefits can be unsettling.

Love and hate are self-explanatory and are both extremes of the emotions people are likely to have around your gamified experience, though you are more likely to see like and dislike. Either way, it is best to aim for them loving your system over hating it!

In Your Design

In the design process you will see later, I put emotions in the BMEM section of my design framework; Behaviours, Motivations, Emotions and Mechanics. The idea is to understand what behaviours you are seeking from the user, what their motivations might be to behave that way (or not) and then what emotions you want them to experience. This is easier in a game as you are creating true virtual worlds for them to play in. In gamification, you are often limited by how you can communicate your vision to the user, but this should not stop you considering emotions anyway! Well worded messages, meaningful rewards, narrative streams and mini games can all go to build strong emotional responses.

How to Use Narrative to Create Deeper Experiences

I like a good story, and how I met Rainbow the Unicorn is a great one. Maybe one day, you will find out all about it. Until then, my master scrawled down some ideas on how to build stories and interactive narratives. Enjoy – or at least pretend to...

Whenever I speak to people in the circles within which I hang out, one of the things I keep hearing is story and narrative. "You have to tell your story", "What is the narrative?", what is the companies' story". To be honest, it drives me a little nuts, but that's by the by. The fact is, these are important things to consider. That said, it got me thinking, is what is the difference between story and narrative?

Story seems to have quite a few definitions. According to the Oxford dictionary, it is:

1. an account of imaginary or real people and events told for entertainment
2. a report of an item of news in a newspaper, magazine, or broadcast
3. an account of past events in someone's life or in the development of something
4. the commercial prospects or circumstances of a company

Whilst narrative is defined as:

1. a spoken or written account of connected events; a story.

So really, story and narrative are pretty much the same things! For me, the most important definition in the context of gamification is number 3 "an account of past events in someone's life or in the development of something". The way I see it, a that the story contains a start, a middle and an end. A narrative is more real time, it describes events as they are happening from the perspective of the person they are happening to. If you consider a game, the narrative would be the way events unfold as you play.

The story will include the backstory and the ongoing plot of the game. That being the case, the story could be the same for each player, whereas the narrative would potentially be unique to each one.

How does this relate to gamification? Well, on the one hand, you could say that everyone has a story, they have a history and they have things happening to them right now, their narratives. All of this goes influences who they are and who they may be in the future. In gamification, we are often looking at influencing or changing behaviour, knowing the story of each person can help inform us how best to engage with and motivate them.

You could look at it even more literally though and create a story and so a narrative for each user to engage with whilst they use your system. This could be especially useful during the on-boarding or scaffolding phases of a design. Take your users through a story, preferably one that changes based on the choices they make and how they wish to go through it. Give them what they need through completing parts of the story. Doing it this way, when done well, will have far more impact on them than giving them points for doing things. The sense of purpose that a story can give is very powerful – even if it is more a short story than an epic!

A picture may be worth a thousand words, but a good story is worth a thousand instruction manuals.

Narrative Atoms

Now that we know a bit more about what narratives are, I want to dive deeper into building narratives and stories, starting with the concept of Narrative atoms.

Narrative atoms are small *units* of narrative or story that can, within the context of the overall narrative, stand alone. That does not mean they need to be completely self-explanatory, just sit comfortably on their own.

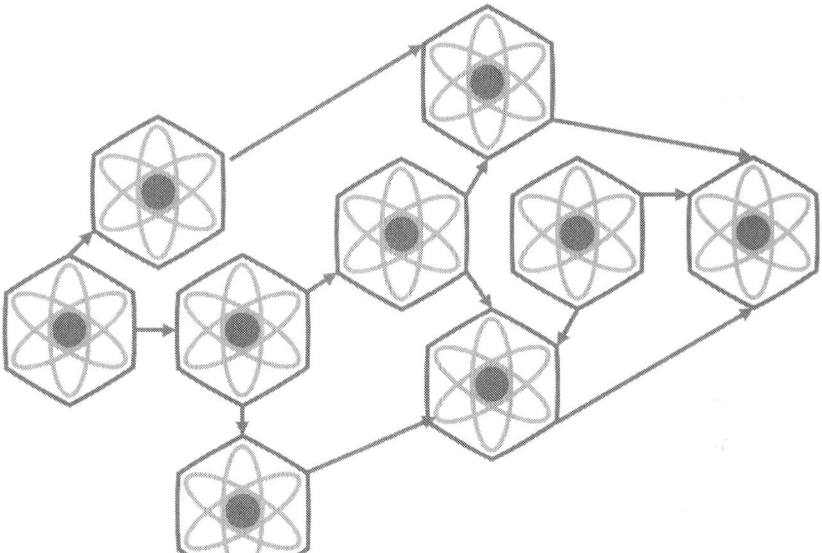

Figure 53 Narrative Atoms

In a standard linear story, each atom would be placed sequentially, so their ability to stand alone is less important. However, in many games the narrative bends and twists and turns in a non-linear way.

For that to work, for a story to make sense as it jumps from A to C to G to B and back again, each section, each narrative atom must be able to hold its own without the need for every other atom to support it.

Take a scenario where a game has more than one option for what can be done after the first scene. Maybe you have a choice of going left or right.

After that, you have more choices and more, but all the while the narrative needs to keep making sense. More than that, it all needs to conclude and not leave the player (unintentionally) wondering what the hell has happened!

Basic Narrative Structure

At their most basic, stories have just three parts. A start, a middle and an end. In traditional media that is straightforward. There are many ideas out there on how to write stories, Joseph Campbell's Hero's Journey / Monomyth [100] gets a lot of attention. I also rather like Kurt Vonnegut concept of Story Shapes [101].

For my purposes when designing simple stories in gamification scenarios I use two simple (and I do mean simple) variations of what I call the Soap Hero's Journey.

The simplest version has four phases. The Calling, The Challenge, The Transformation and The Resolution. The second version adds The Twist after The Transformation. I'll go into more detail later but suffice to say these are not much different from the simple concept of a story having a start a middle and an end!

Bonding Narrative Atoms

Back to narrative atoms. Each atom should have a start a middle and an end. This is how they can stand on their own if needed. As I say, in a linear story this is less important, however, if you are creating a branching narrative it is essential.

The first thing you need to know in a non-linear narrative is obvious, how it will begin. This sounds simple, but you could have multiple starting points for your game's character or characters. After that, you will certainly have many parts to the middle, some the player will see, and some the player might not on the first play through. Finally, there may well be multiple places for the story to end.

As the player will be able to navigate through the story in multiple ways, you must know how each branch fits together and how each choice the player makes can affect the outcome of their story.

This is where considering narrative atoms can help. If each atom has its own start, middle and end it is easier to jump in and out of them at will. As you knit the story together, you can pass events from each atom onto the next one, ensuring that character and plot progression or alteration is kept consistent, without having to create vast quantities of alternative narrative to account for every choice.

An Example of Simple Narrative Atoms

Start

You are in the woods. Ahead of you, there is a fork in the road. You can go left or right. What do you want to do?

- **Go Left**
  - At the fork in the forest, you take the left turn. Ahead of you is a giant monster. It reminds you of ones you used to read about as a child. This is what you had prepared for and you know what you must do. As the beast charges at you, you remember that there is a weak spot on its back, just between its shoulders. All you must do is get your sword in there.
- **You win**
  - The fight with the monster will go down in history and the scar that it has left on your cheek will only add to the legend. You can get behind the beast, finding higher ground to attack the weak spot between its shoulders. Once you are sure it was dead, you take its giant teeth as a trophy and continue on the path towards home.

- **You lose**
    - The fight with the monster will go down in history, but sadly you will be but a footnote. You can get behind the beast, finding higher ground to attack the weak spot between its shoulders, you lunge just a moment too late and are caught by the beast. The last thing you hear is the snap of your neck.
- **Go Right**
    - At the fork in the forest, you take the right turn. The sun is shining, and the birds are singing in the trees. As you walk, you pick flowers from the path and collect them in your bag. After several hours of blissful and uneventful travel, you reach home.

Home

After your journey, you are elated to be home. Your family is waiting to see you, your children eager to see what you have bought them from your travels.

- **If you fought the beast**
    - The fight with the monster has taken its toll and your wife is concerned about your cheek, but before she can speak about it, you produce the monster's teeth from your bag and proudly hand them to the children.

- **If you didn't fight the beast**
  - You turn to your wife and offer her the flowers from your bag, now tied into a beautiful bouquet. For the children, you sit them down to tell them a wonderful story of a hero who must fight a monster in the forest.
  - With your children happy and your wife just pleased to have you home, you settle in by the fire and sleep peacefully.

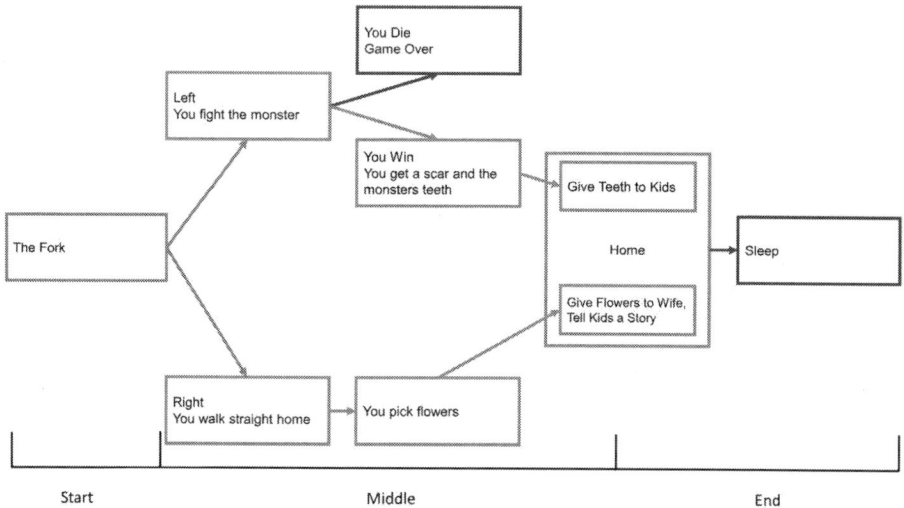

Figure 54 Boy Meets Monster, Boy Kills Monster

Each section of the story can stand up on its own, given the context. Each atom explains itself and resolves itself whilst being able to bond with the next part.

Of course, this is very simple and most non-linear narratives will require each atom to have multiple bonding points, where the story can link to other atoms whilst still making sense, passing on critical information to change key parts of the next atom.

For instance, in our little story, if you fight the monster, you could choose to allow the player to then turn back and take the path where they can pick flowers. This would add an extra bond to the monster fight atom and allow the player to experience both parts of the potential endings – giving the wife flowers and the children the teeth.

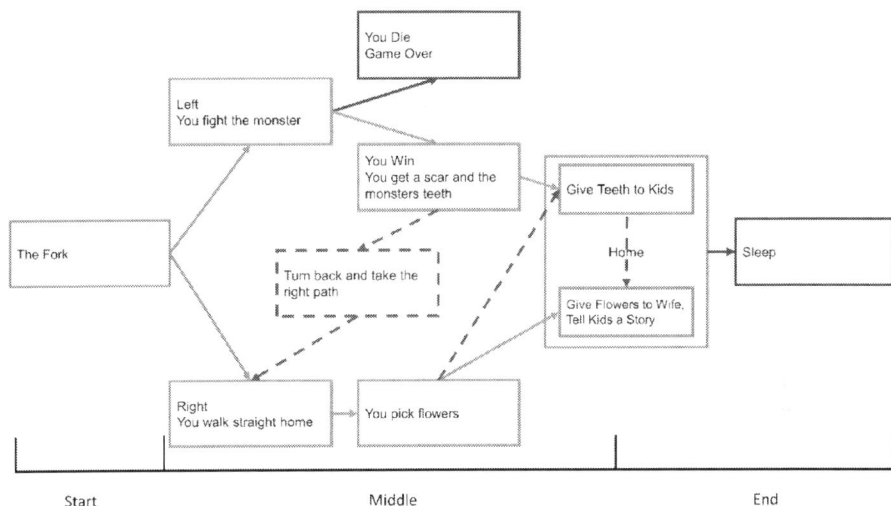

Figure 55 Boy Meets Monster, Boy Kills Monster Again

The key is to make sure that each atom can be as self-sufficient in the narrative as possible and that you only must pass essential information to the next atom to make the story continue to be coherent.

Learning from Games: Her Story & Gone Home

Her Story is the fabulous creation of Sam Barlow. You take the role of investigator, reviewing police archive video footage of a British woman accused of murder. You can access the footage in any order you like, gleaning more clues and information with every video you watch. Sometimes the videos will not make sense until you find the video that came before it, others give you all you need in just a few seconds of footage. The joy is discovering how the story fits together, jumping back and forward through the timeline. New snippets of information give you new ideas on what to search in the archive, leading to many "Ahahaa" moments.

The second is a well-loved game, *Gone Home* from The Fullbright Company, which is a brilliant lesson in narrative design. Like Her Story, Gone Home tells the story in small atoms - fragments of what happened in the house you are exploring. Each scrap of paper, audio recording or newspaper clipping adds something to the story.

Both experiences, whilst seemingly disjointed, eventually build up a deep and fascinating narrative. Each atom may not seem to be relevant but may combine with another atom to unlock a key plot element or answer to a puzzle. In each case, you do not necessarily have to see everything to complete the game, but to gain full understanding, it does help! You also don't have to see everything in chronological order, but it can help.

The lesson is that using narrative atoms can help you create incredibly deep narrative experiences that don't have to follow any path, giving people an opportunity to discover the whole picture in their own unique way!

Meaningful Choice

Heavy Rain. That was the name of the game that first made me understand that meaningful choices could take a game to new levels of immersiveness.

If you have never heard of it, Heavy Rain was a PS3 exclusive in 2010 from game makers Quantic Dream. You played the roles of several people through a convoluted mystery. There was the father who had lost his son, the private eye, the reporter and the FBI agent all linked to the mysterious Origami Killer. As the story unfolded, you had to decide how each character acted, how they handled conversations and what choices they made.

What made this so special was that choices all had consequences. Make the wrong one, and a character could die. Your choices dictated what parts of the story you saw and how it ended. Every decision was critical to how your game played out. In fact, in an interview David Cage, the director of the game, said that he wanted people to only ever play the game once. That way their experience would be unique. When they discussed it with others, they would then find out there were whole sections of the game that they had never seen – so each person's playthrough would be unique to them.

More recently games like Walking Dead and The Wolf Among Us from TellTale Games have taken this approach to choices within their games. Each choice you make feels like there is weight behind it, they feel like they have consequences.

My experience is that people like to feel their choices have meaning, they also like to feel that they have choices in the first place. When you look at my User Types or the RAMP framework, Autonomy is one of the key motivators – especially for the Free Spirit type. That does not mean they are the only ones who are motivated by some level of autonomy. If we feel that we have no freedom to move, to choose and be in control of our own destiny – we feel constrained and disengaged from the experience.

When creating your gamified or game-based solution you should try to build meaningful choices in. The ideal is that choices change the outcomes of the experience, but even if they just *feel* as though they have meaning that can be enough.

If you have a game-like solution, allow users to choose their own way to play the game. Let them solve problems in multiple ways. In narratives, allow them to choose how to answer questions or where they go next in the narrative (that's why I love choose your own adventure style narratives!). In pure gamification, allow users to choose what they do next. If it is a learning experience, let them make their own decisions about what they learn next.

If that level of freedom is not possible, then you should, at least, make it *feel* like there are choices and that they affect outcomes. The trick there is to make sure they can't go back and repeat their actions – thus discovering their original choice did not affect the outcome after all. I have seen this in a lot of games. It feels like you are making decisions that change how the game will play, but then on replays, it turns out that the game would always funnel you down to the same conclusion no matter how you played!

Narrative Choice Architecture in Gamification

Combining the concepts of narrative atoms and meaningful choice, we begin to explore narrative choice architecture, where each choice makes a real difference or at least appears to. Here I discuss a few different approaches.

When you sit down with a book, you start at the start and then read every page until you get to the end (unless it is a choose your own adventure...). The only choice the reader gets is whether to start the book and read it all the way through or not.

Figure 56 Simple Architecture

Games allow you to do more than that for the player. Games allow you to give the player much higher levels of autonomy or agency.

For a sandbox game, like Minecraft, this is quite simple – the player has total freedom as there is no actual end game. There are still choices to be made, but they are not driven by story. How big will my house be, do I dig for gold, do I make a roller coaster? Rather than designing a choice architecture, you just give the player the tools to support them.

However, games with some form of narrative can be made much more interesting by allowing some level of agency beyond the simple "start at the start and end at the end" idea.

Fake Choice Architecture

One option that you see is to give players "fake" options or choices. They get the choice to turn left or right at a junction, but really both paths will eventually lead to the same ending. They may experience different events taking the left rather than the right, but the end goal is the same, as we discussed in our *Boy Meets Monster* example earlier.

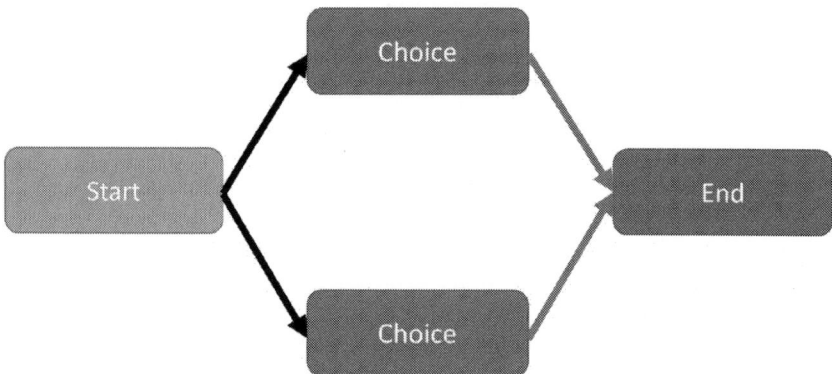

Figure 57 Simple Fake Choice

This sort of architecture works well in games that are only designed to be played once or where the gameplay is more important than the narrative. An example that comes to mind is that of older first-person shooters. You could choose where to go on some maps or what your path was, but you always ended up in the same place. However, the choice had weight and meaning as it altered the tactics you would use each time you ran through the level.

There is nothing wrong with this sort of architecture if you can make the choices feel that they are meaningful and have significance to the game. You can also get very complex, with multiple twists and turns before you come to the inevitable conclusion.

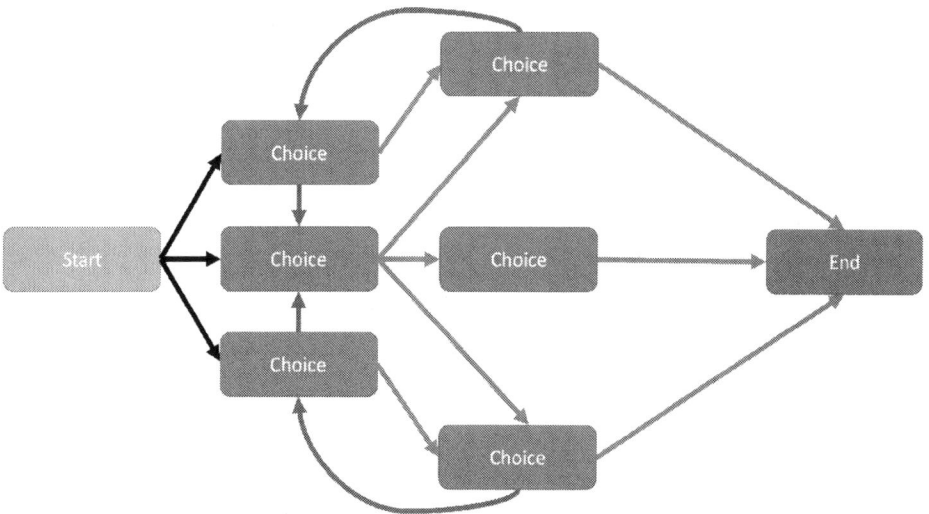

Figure 58 Complex Fake Choice

A game that makes good use of this would be Tell Tale's Walking Dead. Every choice you make alters the way the game will play. Who will live, who will die, how people react to you. However, the conclusion is always just about the same. You may have fewer people left and there may be some strained relationships, but the end of the game is the same each time.

Real Choice Architecture

The alternative to the fake choice architecture is real choice architecture. Here the player's actions have real significance to how the game will play. A simple example would be the player back at the junction in boy meets monster. They can go left or right. Either choice in this architecture gives a totally different outcome for the player. The choice they make has real meaning to the rest of the game.

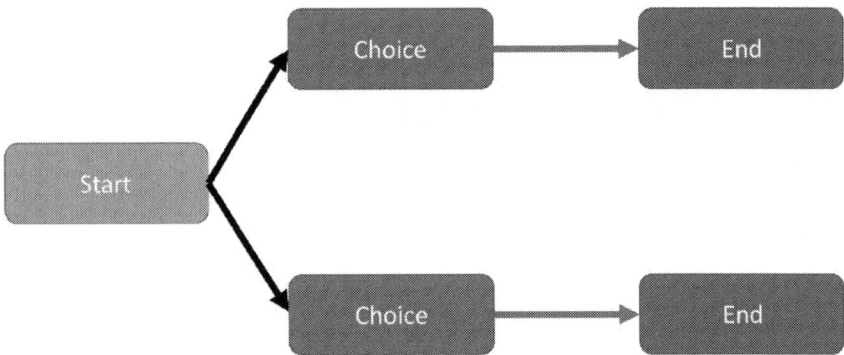

Figure 59 Simple Real Choice

The significance can be less obvious than that of course. If you think about RPG games and how you can interact with non-playable characters (NPCs).

Very often the choices you make in your dialog will determine how the NPC will react to you not just in that conversation, but later in the game. A simple choice to be aggressive could turn a whole faction against you, altering the whole balance of the game. Suddenly seemingly simple interaction become deeply meaningful to the game.

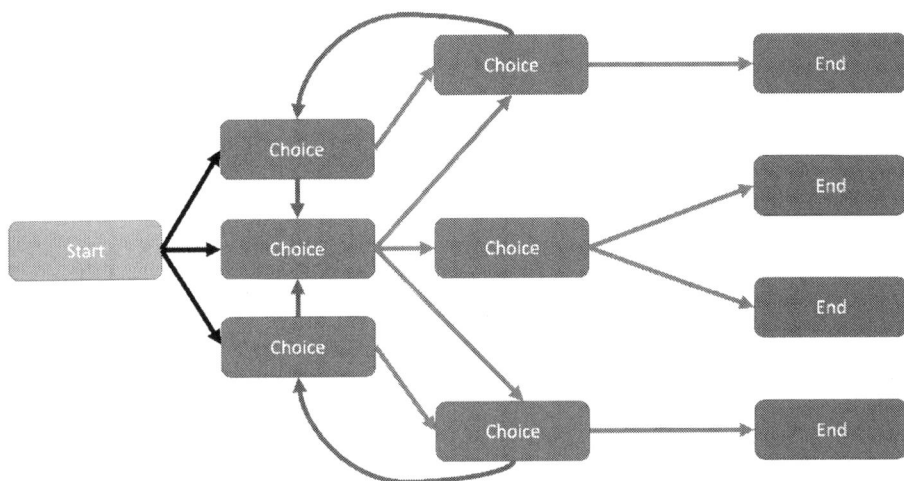

Figure 60 Complex Real Choice

Heavy Rain was a great example of this more complex choice architecture. There were many endings that could only be seen if you made specific sets of choices along the way.

Choice Architecture and Gamification

In gamification, it appears the choice architecture is straightforward. You need users to perform certain tasks, for which there will be some sort of reward. However, it doesn't need to be that simple. You can design the user journey so that they can make choices along the way.

The outcome is likely going to need to be the same for each user, but if it is a gamified system, the likelihood is they will only experience it once anyway! Add things in that are just for fun, but like a video game side mission, are totally optional.

Create simple narratives and stories that are affected by certain decisions but make them have some effect on the outcome. I remember taking a "gamified" course. At the start, you chose your team and along the way you had the option to collect certain items. It seemed great, until the end – at which point it turned out that none of the choices you made had any influence on the outcome at all. All it had to do was unlock a simple message or change the last image, but no – nothing. I have no idea what the course was teaching, all I remember is the outrage I felt at being tricked into doing more than was essential because it felt like my choices may have some importance!

"Choices do not need to lead to alternative endings, just alternative experiences."

The Soap Hero's Journey

Now that we have an idea of how to construct the individual moments of the narrative, we need to have some idea of how it will all come together in a real story. I mentioned the simple narrative model I often use, the soap hero's journey. I use this because it is easy to remember and is also the core of most short storytelling arcs – such as soap operas.

A Soap Hero's Journey

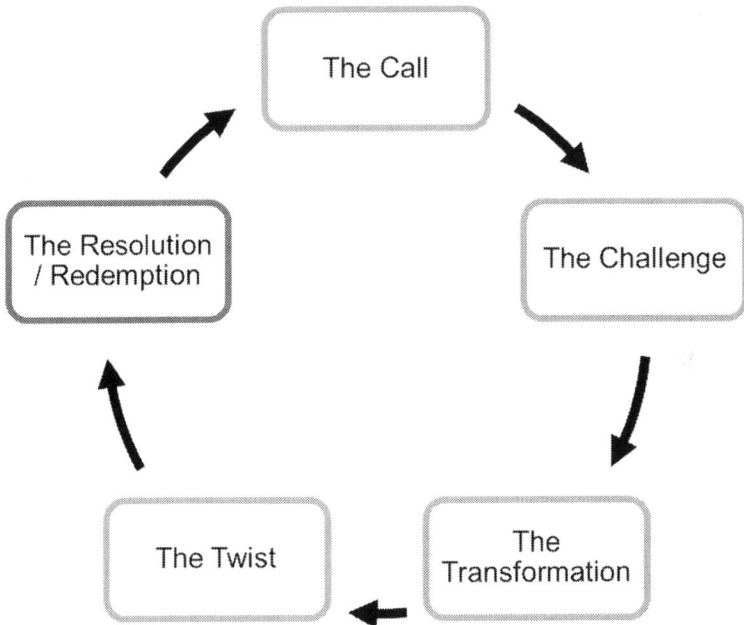

The Call

The Challenge

The Resolution / Redemption

The Twist

The Transformation

Figure 61 The Soap Hero's Journey

- **The Call**
  - The event that triggers the characters to start the journey
  - Plot
- **The Challenge**
  - Conflicts, difficulties, tasks that the characters must overcome.
- **The Transformation**
  - The change that happens to the characters as they learn to overcome the obstacles
- **The Twist (optional)**
  - Often before the full resolution, there is a twist that forces the hero to practice their new skills or re-evaluate something they have learned during the transformation.
- The Resolution
  - How all the characters finally overcome or rationalise the challenges.
  - Uses all their new knowledge.

This is nice and simple and works well with the concept of narrative atoms, keeping each atom of the story simple. This is how soaps like EastEnders do it, keeping each episode a short, self-contained story, whilst still having character progression and plot progression that can feed into the next episode. That way, those who have not seen the soap before can pick it up easily, whilst those that have been watching for years can enjoy it at a deeper level.

Below is a silly example of an EastEnders plot put into the Soap Hero's Journey.

- **The Call**
  - Cat Moon has run away, but Alfie doesn't know why.
  - He must find her.
- **The Challenge**
  - First, he must find out where she has gone.
  - Then He must find her
  - He must find out why she left
  - Finally, he must bring her home
- **The Transformation**
  - He finds out from her friend that she ran away to Spain because he was too controlling
  - Realises he must change how he feels about her past and grow up about it
- **The Twist**
  - Gets to Spain and discovers it was all a lie, she was still in Walford!
- **The Resolution / Redemption**
  - Finds Cat
  - Apologises to her and tells her he loves her
  - Convinces her he has changed
  - Brings her home and discovers she is pregnant
  - Duff Duffs...

As you can see from the ending there, this narrative atom can neatly bond onto the next episode!

Combining the concepts of Narrative Atoms and a simple story structure like the Soap Hero's Journey, you can build strong narratives that can bend and twist to your heart's content. Just keep on top of character and plot development between atoms, and you will be fine!

Keeping It Real in Fantasy Worlds

Whilst we are on the subject of narrative, it makes sense to think a little more about the workings of fantasy worlds. Richard Bartle once raised an interesting point about certain fantasy-based shows and games after watching *Game of Thrones*. His complaint was that even in fantasy worlds, there need to be rules and those rules need to be stuck to.

Anything that is not explained by the new rules of the fantasy world should then default to the rules of the real world. One example he gave was that of Sam in *Game of Thrones*. Despite a very active lifestyle in GoT, he doesn't lose as much weight as you might expect if it were the real world, and there is no explanation for why that may be.

You can understand and accept the existence of magic and dragons, because the narrative introduces them early on – so they are established as part of the rules of the world. However, lack of weight loss in Sam's instance seems to be very unlikely as no rules have been introduced that would explain how weight loss works differently in the world of Westeros.

It is like standing at a pedestrian crossing and upon pressing the button, all the cars turn in to cabbages.

There is no reason for this to happen, no explanation in the rules of our world that would lead you to believe that this could happen, so it would stand out to you as being a bit odd!

This brings me to play and gamification.

As I have introduced earlier, play has fluid *meta-rules*. However, the big "no no" in play, especially amongst children, is introducing a new rule that is unexpected or does not make sense within the context of the current game.

Playing "Rock, Paper, Scissors" and choosing a bazooka is a sure-fire way to get tears from a young child! That is not to say that you can't play like that. My kids play "Rock, Paper, Anything" and you get some truly odd arguments over whether Harry Potter could beat a space tank.... However, this is fine, because they set the expectation that anything goes at the start – not half way through.

World Building in Gamification

In gamification, we don't spend enough time considering the worlds we create because we don't see them as worlds in that sense. Often, they are just pictures and narratives that link content together. We forget that the narrative alone creates a world for the user to engage with and that world needs to be consistent and have rules just like any other virtual or fantasy world does!

The first few screens set the expectation for the rest of the experience. If you start with all singing all dancing graphics, the user will expect those throughout. If the narrative talks about being a mild-mannered account in an office much like the player's own, they won't be expecting a magical warlock to suddenly appear. That is not to say that you can't do that, but the rest of the narrative needs to explain it and reset the expectations of the player.

The Unintended Consequences of Minor Details!

When creating a gamified solution, spend time thinking about the rules of any worlds you are creating. If you are creating a theme, what would the expected rules be? If you have a medieval them, your players would not expect or accept aeroplanes being in the narrative. If the players are trapped in a building, they would not expect there to be a well in the middle of the 5th floor.

You need to be consistent and mindful of the expectations you set early on and how they will affect the player's experience. The best case is that unexplainable events will seem odd, the worst is that it will break them out of any immersive state you have managed to induce!

Don't waste all that effort by tripping yourself up on the unintended consequences of seemingly minor details!

There is a great a trope of storytelling linked to minor details called *Chekov's Gun*

Anton Chekov, a Russian playwright, stated that if an element of the story is not necessary, remove it. He said;

"One must never place a loaded rifle on the stage if it isn't going to go off. It's wrong to make promises you don't mean to keep." [102]

Keep it simple people!

How to Create Playful Experiences

When I finally become the Master, my first job (after a little bit of vengeance...) will be to use the ideas in this chapter to create more playful environments for people. It pains me to say, but my Master's concepts here can help you understand how to create playfulness.

Emergence is a well-known concept in game design. Emergent gameplay comes when players interact with the mechanics of the game creating situations that have not been deliberately designed.

For instance, the game may offer several tools to solve a puzzle but allow the player to use them in any way they see fit. If the puzzle requires you to reach an item that is high up, there could be an infinite number of ways to get it. Use a grappling hook, build a tower, make a jetpack and so on.

Unintentional emergence comes when players use the game world in a way that the designers had never intended. Take for instance a racing game. The idea is to race from point A to point B as fast as possible. However, if players instead decide to chase each other and try and knock each other off the course, that is unintentional emergence. The game designer had not set that up as a deliberate way of playing – however, the mechanics and the rules allow it to happen.

Minecraft is a fabulous example of both intentional and unintentional emergence in a game environment. Notch created a world with very specific rules that governed how it worked and simple mechanics to play with. Whilst there is a simple core goal, survive, there is so much more that can be done. You must collect wood for instance. You can do this by hand, but once you have some wood you can create a simple tool to help. Tools that are more complex can be created as you collect more raw materials.

However, there is no one solution to each situation in which you find yourself. Your first shelter can be made in any way you wish out of any material you can find. In effect, you can do almost anything the environmental rules will allow, whilst playing the core game of "survival".

The unintentional emergence this freedom has born is unlike anything I have previously seen, possibly except for *Second Life*. People create new games and new ways to play almost every day it seems. From simple races to *Hunger Games* style multiplayer events. They have created roller coasters, well-known landmarks, computers, recreations of large areas of Rome, films and even entire sections of the world from *Game of Thrones* and more. This is part of what has made it one of the most popular games of all time!

Figure 62 Kings Landing from Game of Thrones

Emergence in Gamification

It may seem that this is not applicable to gamification. In gamification, we are usually trying to drive certain outcomes or encourage a particular set of behaviours. However, why should that be all that we are doing? If you look at a gamified system, it contains a set of simple rules or mechanics with which the user interacts. In gamification emergence is often considered cheating, but can't it be more?

Take the unintentional situation that can emerge when the rules allow for an unexpected behaviour. You assign points to people for inviting other people into the system. The intention of the design would be simple. They would expect people to behave in a way they would consider "acceptable", so maybe inviting 1 to 20 people. However, the rules and mechanics allow for much more than that. A user could invite hundreds of people. They could create a script that invites thousands of people.

Is that cheating? If the rules never stated that there was a limit to the number of people each user could invite, and the mechanics of the system allow it to happen – then no. Really, it is emergence. A user has taken the rules and the mechanics and done something unexpected, but totally allowed!

The real question is how can we make use of this? Well, the person who wrote a script to email thousands of people, showed some serious initiative and potentially some coding skills that may have been previously unknown to the company.

As a gamification designer, we could allow a lack of rigidity in our rules to try to encourage people to come up with creative solutions to the problems we present them.

We must be a little careful that creativity is not seen as cheating though – what is fair game for some is often seen as cheating by others. Where a Player user type may feel that paying for items to get further is fine, an Achiever type may well feel that is cheating.

Another good example is people creating social groups and trading votes, answers, ideas and the like. Again, some may see it as unethical – but if the rules allow it – it is fair game!

Creating a Play-Like Environment

As discussed already, in play, the goals are often less defined or not consciously apparent. Whilst there may be rules that dictate how play progresses: social rules, physical rules and so on, they are not there to be deliberately challenging or to make play harder.

To make activities more play-like, you need to drop system rules and goals as much as possible, whilst creating a safe environment.

Part of what makes play so compelling is that there is a reduced level of real danger to the participants. Animals playing do not tend to hurt each other deliberately; they know that it is play. Kids playing are not afraid of the tower they are building falling. It may be annoying, but it is not going to get them in trouble or cause any real issues. Even in games, dying is often just a matter of losing a life – you can start again.

More importantly is that failure leads to learning and improving performance next time, but only if failure does not lead to a harmful punishment.

In the real world, this all seems a little unrealistic. What company is going to let people just go off and do their own thing without fear of failure? Well, Google for one. You may remember the 80/20 rule they made so famous a few years ago [103]? The idea was that 20% of an employee's time could be spent working on their own ideas and concepts. They did not have to produce anything, as long as they were trying. There was no punishment if their experiments failed, but if they succeeded, they could find a great deal of support. Products like Gmail came out of this, just as an example.

It may not seem like play, but it has play-like elements. There are no system/company set goals (Make a product). There are no rules set by the system/company that make it harder (only use the letter E once per line of code) or system/company defined obstacles (Do it by Friday and within budget). There is a safe environment as failure is not punished and there is no expectation of success. Also, and this is massively important, they had autonomy – they could choose what they wanted to work on and were trusted to get on with it.

I have deliberately used the phrase "Play-Like" here. This is not play, but it is closer to play than work would normally be. Play and Games have one important thing that makes them what they are, the concept I introduced earlier – Lusory or a playful attitude and mindset. Really, it is an exercise in learning from play, just as we learn from games in gamification - Playification?

Here are five simple tips for creating play-like systems:

1. The system should have no defined goals (counter to creating gamified solutions!)
2. The system should have no defined obstacles
3. Trust the user
4. Provide a safe environment to fail within
5. Give the user freedom and autonomy to explore the system and push the boundaries

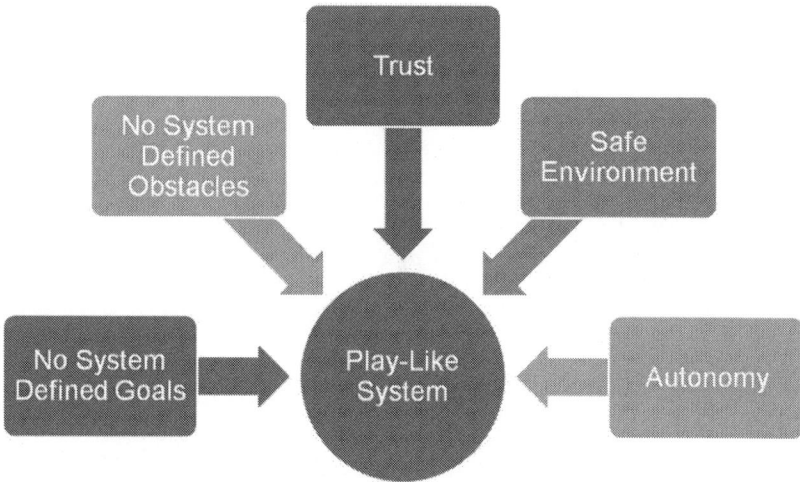

Figure 63 Framework for creating Play-Like systems

How to Handle Cheating

I never cheat, but that is not to say that some won't feel that my methods are cheating. At times, cheating is a matter of context and subjective consideration. Cheating or not, I always make sure I understood the rules and where they can be bent.

A question that is often asked is – "what do you do about cheating in a gamified system?"

Let's look at a real example of observed behaviour within a gamified system. In this case – my blog! I had a trivial layer type of gamification on my blog that rewarded users for simple actions. It was there as a bit of fun for users who wished to engage. However, it did have one user pushing the boundaries of "good" behaviour. Let's look at the user journey for this person.

At the beginning, they came in as a Player (Consumer type specifically). They were looking to play with the points and badges system, whilst learning how the system all worked. This was the *on-boarding* phase of their journey.

Next, they began to enjoy learning from and exploring the content, putting them into the intrinsic "Free Spirit" and "Achiever" types. This was the *immerse* phase.

However, the *mastery* phase took a sharp turn. Rather than staying on for intrinsic reasons, the game took over. Part of the reason for this was a lack of new and challenging content. When asked, the user stated, *"The new materials started to dry up, I had no new activity to do, and still I was way behind the number one player"*. So rather than being there to learn more about gamification from the content, they decided to learn how the game system worked and how to exploit it. They started a new journey, this time not just as a Player/Exploiter type, but also as a full Disruptor. They wanted to prove the system was wrong whilst still beating it. They sat between Destroyer and Improver.

Is It Cheating?

When I talked to them about this on Facebook, one of the issues they raised was the fact that as well as no new materials, they felt unfairly treated by the system. For over a month, a bug had meant they were not getting points for activities. Therefore, they decided that it was fair to *game* the system to recover the points they felt owed. At first, I thought this was a little bit like not being given a refund for something in a shop and then going and stealing from them until you feel the debt is paid.

The thing is; they had not really cheated. The system allowed the user to behave in this way and there were no explicit rules written stating that this sort of behaviour would lead to some kind of penalty. The trouble is that we tend to believe that everyone in the world will behave and adhere to certain social norms; the truth is that this is not the case. Whilst the user may have spoiled the game for others who were playing "fairly", they got what they wanted – position on the leaderboard.

How do you handle this? The first thing is to make sure that if you do not want it to happen, the system does not allow it. One option is to have a system that makes repeated behaviours in a day worth less each time. This makes it pointless to continue spamming. The other is to state clearly, how you expect players to behave and have in place a system to penalise or ban offenders.

Also, remember that different people perceive cheating differently. Professor Richard Bartle has a great presentation on this. [104]

He once said that it is not possible to cheat in a gamified system as you can in a game. In a game, most voluntarily enter a social contract with other players, one that has implicit expectations of behaviour, courteous conduct.

It can be argued that with some gamified systems, you do not do this, especially if users are "forced" into them. Whilst this is true of some systems, enterprise being the biggest case for this, a system such as CaptainUp (a plug and play gamification extension for websites) is voluntary. No one is forcing you to play, so should you be expected to enter the same social contract of implicit expectations as a game?

I think the answer is yes. Will everyone want to? This whole section proves the answer to that is "No – of course not!"

Lessons Learned

Make sure that the system does not allow for cheating in the first place – test, test and test some more.

Create a simple set of rules that are highly visible to your users. This will give more weight to decisions made about who is "cheating". You cannot break the rules if there are none!

You need constant fresh content. If you have nothing but the game, then people will just play or leave – they will not stay to learn, as there is nothing to learn! This is where user-generated content can be a huge boost to a system.

In the end, I removed the user. They were no longer of value to the site and had lost my trust to some extent. Also, their score was unattainable for most players, so was off-putting to them.

The other interesting thing is that in a weird way, the gamification worked perfectly. The user in question has obviously learned a great deal as they explored the site. I just had no *end game* planned for them!

How to See it From the User's Perspective

Don't get lost with introspection during your design. Keep in mind that the user may see the solution very differently to you. At least that's how it seems when I think about my Master's training methods.

How the User Views It All

As a gamification designer, it can be very easy to become caught up in the intricacies of the system. The feedback mechanics, the game mechanics, the economy and the cleverness of it all. It is also easy to think, "This is going to be great" when you have a new idea and then spend too long making the idea real.

What we need to do is step back from time to time and ask; "How will this actually impact the user"?

For example, you have a fabulous animation that you want to make use of. It fits the overall theme of the gamified solution you are building, and you think that it adds a little bit of playfulness to break up part of the process. Great. However, what does it really give the end user? If it is used once and adds some greater value to the process they are going through by giving a new understanding or insight – then brilliant.

If it gives the user a break from a particularity complex part of the process, then okay. However, if it sits there and forces them to watch it, possibly more than once with no option to skip – step away from the idea.

You see, you think it is awesome and fun, but the user sees it as something that is getting between them and the end of the process they are going through. They do not really care that you spent 20 hours perfecting the animation. They have no interest that you missed your child's birthday party to add this bit of light relief just for them. They only care that it added time to a process or, interfered with it.

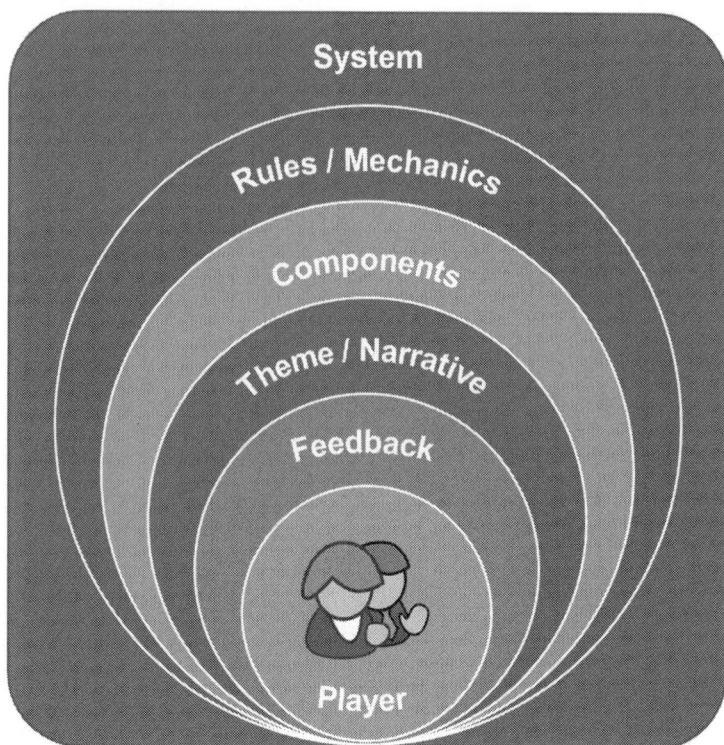

Figure 64 The user doesn't care!

How I see it, the player is most impacted by the feedback your system provides. This is what will frame the experience for them and what gives them their sense of progress, achievement, motivation etc.

Feedback can be anything from the word "correct" on a test to the outputs of a full virtual economy and the screen flashing and dancing!

After that, the theme or narrative. Whilst this may not be important to all, it will affect the user in different ways – especially if it is handled badly, think "Skip" button whenever you are using anything that can be voluntarily watched!

Components are objects like progress bars and the like. Whilst they are part of feedback, the design, bells and whistles of them is not always that important to the user – just as long as they work and don't interfere!

Finally, the rules and the mechanics. As we have seen in previous chapters, these are what makes the system work. They define how the system will feedback based on the user's actions. The user does not care about this – they will only notice the existence of the mechanics and rules if they interfere with completing their assigned tasks or don't work properly!

Sadly, the fact of the matter is, the user does not care how clever the designers were. They just want a system that works and that is usable. As a designer, your problems are not the user's problems. However, the user's problems are most definitely your problems!

Gamification Mechanics and Elements

Here are some elements that my *Master* feels support his User Types and can improve your gamified systems. I rather like Anarchy for disruptors...

Earlier in the book, I introduced game mechanics. Now, let's looks at some gamification mechanics, elements and ideas that you can use in your system. These are broken down into general (can be used to support anyone), schedules (some examples of reward schedules that have already been covered) and what User Type they most support.

General	
	On-boarding/Tutorials No one uses manuals anymore! Help people get used to your system with a nice tutorial or a gentle introduction on how everything works.
	Signposting Sometimes, even the best people need to be pointed in the right direction. Signpost next actions to help smooth early stages of a journey. Use "just in time" cues to help users who are stuck.
	Loss Aversion No one likes to lose anything they have earned. Fear of losing status, friends, points, achievements, possessions, progress etc. can be a powerful reason for people to act.

	Progress/Feedback Progress and feedback come in many forms and have many mechanisms available. All User Types need some sort of measure of progress or feedback, but some types work better than others do.
	Theme Give your gamification a theme, often linked with narrative. Can be anything from company values to werewolves. Add a little fantasy; just make sure users can make sense of it.
	Narrative/Story Tell your story and let people tell theirs. Use gamification to strengthen understanding of your story by involving people. Think like a writer!
	Curiosity/Mystery Box Curiosity is a strong force. Not everything has to be fully explained, a little mystery may encourage people in new directions.
	Time Pressure Reducing the amount of time people must do things can focus them on the problem. It can also lead to different decisions.

	Scarcity Making something rare can make it even more desirable.
	Strategy Make people think about what they are doing, why they are doing it and how it might affect the outcomes of the game.
	Flow Getting the perceived levels of challenge and skill just right can lead to a state of Flow. Balance is the key.
	Consequences If the user gets things wrong, what are the consequences? Do they lose a life, points or items they have earned?
	Investment When people invest time, effort, emotions or money, they will value the outcomes even more.

Schedules

Random Rewards

Surprise and delight people with unexpected rewards. Keep them on their toes and maybe even make them smile.

Fixed Reward Schedule

Reward people based on defined actions and events. First activity, level up, progression. Useful during on-boarding and to celebrate milestone events.

Time Dependent Rewards

Events that happen at specific times (birthdays etc.) or are only available for a set period of time (e.g. come back each day for a reward). Users must be there to benefit.

Socialiser

Guilds/Teams

Let people build close-knit guilds or teams. Small groups can be much more effective than large sprawling ones. Create platforms for collaboration but also pave the way for team-based competitions.

Social Network

Allow people to connect and be social with an easy to use and accessible social network. It is can be more fun to play with other people than to play on your own.

Social Status

Status can lead to greater visibility for people, creating opportunities to create new relationships. It can also feel good. You can make use of feedback mechanics such as leaderboards and certificates.

Social Discovery

A way to find people and to be found is essential for building new relationships. Matching people based on interests and status can all help get people started.

	Social Pressure People often don't like feeling they are the odd one out. In a social environment, this can be used to encourage people to be like their friends. Can de-motivate if expectations are unrealistic.
	Competition Competition gives people a chance to prove themselves against others. It can be a way to win rewards but can also be a place where new friendships and relationships are born.

	# Free spirit
	Exploration Give your Free Spirits room to move and explore. If you are creating virtual worlds, consider that they will want to find the boundaries and give them something to find.

	Branching Choices Let the user choose their path and destiny. From multiple learning paths to responsive narratives. Remember, choice must be (or at least feel) meaningful to be most effective and appreciated.
	Easter Eggs Easter eggs are a fun way to reward and surprise people for just having a look around. For some, the harder they are to find, the more exciting it is!
	Unlockable/Rare Content Add to the feeling of self-expression and value, by offering unlockable or rare content for Free Spirits to use. Linked to Easter eggs and exploration as well as achievement.
	Creativity Tools Allow people to create their own content and express themselves. This may be for personal gain, for pleasure or to help other people (teaching materials, levels, gear, FAQ etc.).
	Customisation Give people the tools to customise their experience. From avatars to the environment, let them express themselves and choose how they will present themselves to others.

Achiever

Challenges

Challenges help keep people interested, testing their knowledge and allowing them to apply it. Overcoming challenges will make people feel they have earned their achievement.

Certificates

Different from general rewards and trophies, certificates are a physical symbol of mastery and achievement. They carry meaning, status and are useful.

Learning/New Skills

What better way to achieve mastery than to learn something new? Give your users the opportunity to learn and expand.

Quests

Quests give users a fixed goal to achieve. Often made up of a series of linked challenges, multiplying the feeling of achievement.

Levels/Progression

Levels and goals help to map a user's progression through a system. It is as important to see where you can go as it is to see where you have been.

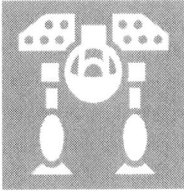

Boss Battles

Boss battles are a chance to consolidate every-thing you have learned and mastered in one epic challenge. Usually, signals the end of the journey – and the beginning of a new one.

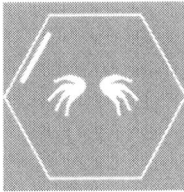

Philanthropists

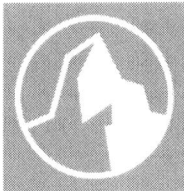

Meaning/Purpose

Some just need to understand the meaning or the purpose of what they are doing (epic or other-wise). For others, they need to feel they are part of something greater than themselves.

	Care-taking Looking after other people can be very fulfilling. Create roles for administrators, moderators, curators etc. Allow users to take a parental role.
	Access Access to more features and abilities in a system can give people more ways to help others and to contribute. It also helps make them feel valued. More meaningful if earned.
	Collect & Trade Many people love to collect things. Give them a way to collect and trade items in your system. Helps build relationships and feelings of purpose and value.
	Gifting/Sharing Allow gifting or sharing of items to other people to help them achieve their goals. Whilst a form of altruism, the potential for reciprocity can be a strong motivator.
	Sharing Knowledge For some, helping other people by sharing knowledge with them is its own reward. Build the ability for people to answer questions and teach others.

	# Player

Points / Experience Points (XP)

Points and XP are feedback mechanics. Can track progress, as well as be used as a way to unlock new things. Award based on achievement or desired behaviour.

Physical Rewards / Prizes

Physical rewards and prizes can promote lots of activity and when used well, can create engagement. Be careful of promoting quantity over quality.

Leaderboards / Ladders

Leaderboards come in different flavours, most commonly relative or absolute. Commonly used to show people how they compare to others and so others can see them. Not for everyone.

Badges / Achievements

Badges and achievements are a form of feedback. Award them to people for accomplishments. Use them wisely and in a meaningful way to make them more appreciated.

	Virtual Economy Create a virtual economy and allow people to spend their virtual currency on real or virtual goods. Look into the legalities of this type of system and consider the long term financial costs!
	Lottery / Game of Chance Lotteries and games of chance are a way to win rewards with very little effort from the user. You have to be in it, to win it though!

	# Disruptor
	Innovation Platform Disruptors think outside the box and boundaries of your system. Give them a way to channel that and you can generate great innovations.
	Voting/Voice Give people a voice and let them know that it is being heard. Change is much easier if everyone is on the same page.

	Development Tools Think modifications rather than hacking and breaking. Let them develop new add-ons to improve and build on the system.
	Anonymity If you want to encourage total freedom and lack of inhibitions, allow your users to remain anonymous. Be very, very careful as anonymity can bring out the worst in people!
	Light Touch Whilst you must have rules, if you are encouraging disruption, apply them with a light touch. See how things play out before jumping in. Keep a watchful eye and listen to the feedback of users.
	Anarchy Sometimes you just must burn it all to the ground and start again. Sit back, throw the rulebook out of the window and see what happens! Consider running short "no rules" events.

Periodic Table of Gamification Elements

#	Symbol	Name	Category
1	Rr	Random Rewards	Rs
2	Fr	Fixed Reward	Rs
3	Td	Time Dependent	Rs
4	Ob	On-boarding	G
5	Si	Signposting	G
6	La	Loss Aversion	G
7	I	Investment	G
8	Pf	Progress / Feedback	G
9	T	Theme	G
10	N	Narrative	G
11	C	Curiosity	G
12	Tp	Time Pressure	G
13	S	Scarcity	G
14	St	Strategy	G
15	F	Flow	G
16	Co	Consequences	G
17	Gt	Guilds / Teams	S
18	Sn	Social Network	S
19	Ss	Social Status	S
20	Sd	Social Discovery	S
21	Sp	Social Pressure	S
22	C	Competition	S
23	Ch	Challenges	A
24	Ce	Certificates	A
25	L	Learning	A
26	Q	Quests	A
27	Lp	Levels / Progression	A
28	Bb	Boss Battles	A
29	E	Exploration	Fs
30	Bc	Branching Choices	Fs
31	Ee	Easter Eggs	Fs
32	U	Unlockables	Fs
33	Ct	Creativity Tools	Fs
34	Cu	Customisation	Fs
35	Ap	Altruistic Purpose	P
36	Cg	Care Taking	P
37	A	Access	P
38	Cn	Collection	P
39	Gs	Gifting / Sharing	P
40	Ks	Knowledge Share	P
41	P	Points	Pl
42	Pr	Prizes	Pl
43	Le	Leaderboards	Pl
44	B	Badges	Pl
45	Ve	Virtual Economy	Pl
46	Lo	Lottery	Pl
47	Ip	Innovation Platform	D
48	V	Voting	D
49	Dt	Development Tools	D
50	A	Anonymity	D
51	Lt	Light Touch	D
52	An	Anarchy	D

Legend:

Rs	Reward Schedule
G	General
S	Socialiser
A	Achiever
Fs	Free Spirit
P	Philanthropist
Pl	Player
D	Disruptor

Learning from Games: Exclusivity & Fortnite

Mid 2018, gaming phenomenon Fortnite ran an event that signalled the end of their 4th season and a whole new set of clues to what may be coming next.

Two weeks prior to the event, players had seen a skull on in-game televisions, which had turned into a countdown – heading towards the 30th of June. The Friday before the event, an in-game message advised players to get into the game on the 30th and look to the sky.

Players who were able to get in then witnessed a rocket launch that tore open an interdimensional rift in the sky.

It may not seem like much, but to players of Fortnite, this was a "Where were you when it happened" type of moment. A moment that will only happen live once. If you were not there, you will never get to experience it properly.

It was exclusive! Its exclusivity created a group of people who shared a particular bond formed on the simple basis of "we were there". It may not seem important, but it is to them in the context of Fortnite.

In gamification it is often easy to lose sight of the fact we are dealing with real people, not just business objectives. They like to feel that those communicating with them, via whatever medium, value them in some way. They also like to feel that they are special!

Implementing Exclusivity in Gamification

There are many ways to create the feeling of exclusivity in your gamification solutions and they don't have to be difficult.

- Taking the time to create Easter eggs that only the most dedicated of players will find is a simple way to create that exclusive feeling for some.

- Adding content that only players who have achieved certain things can access. For instance, if you have an avatar in your system, create a special hat that only players who have completed everything by the second Tuesday of the month get to wear.

- Taking a leaf out of Fortnite's book, create events that only happen the once, invite only or time sensitive.

- Creating communication campaigns that target certain players is another. How many emails have you had that say things like "You are invited" or "You have been chosen". You know that that email has gone to thousands of other people, but it feels personal, special. You were chosen, you are part of the special group.

- Build up curiosity by hinting at things, like the TV screens in Fortnite.

- Create anticipation!

PLANNING AND IMPLEMENTING YOUR

GAMIFICATION DESIGN

Gamification Design Framework

My Master keeps making new frameworks. Whilst he and Rainbow Unicorn conversed on "holiday", he once again changed his mind on how to best build gamified solutions. What follows is his latest Gamification Design Framework. Make of it what you will...

Over the years, I have come up with various design frameworks. In the first edition of this book, I included one called the GAME framework, I have since refined and improved this significantly and created the Gamification Design Framework, outlined here.

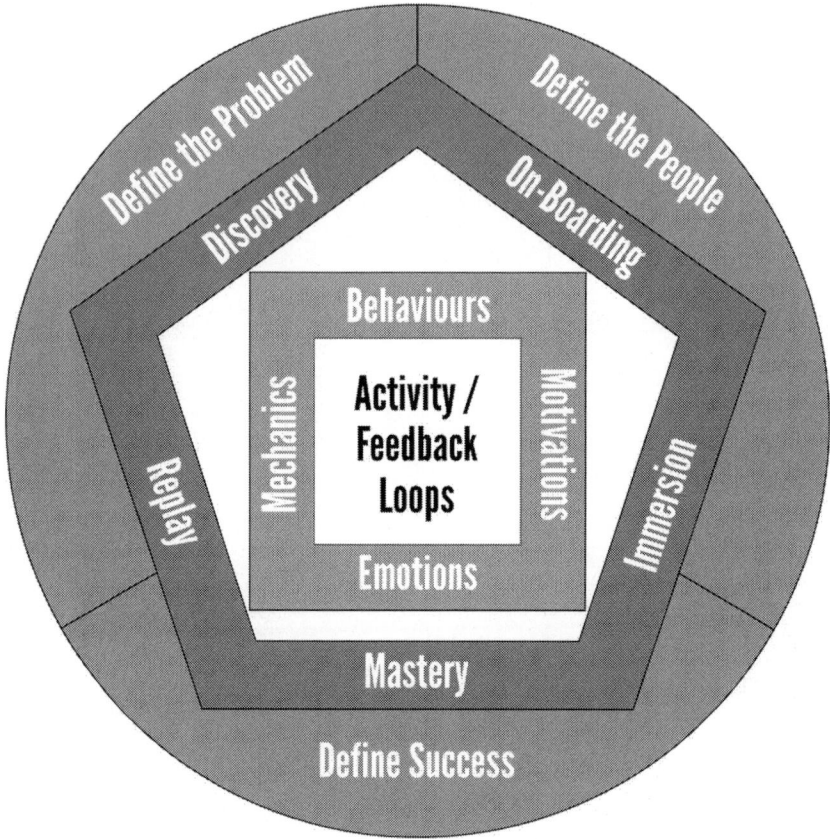

Figure 65 The Gamification Design Framework

It consists of three main phases; Define, Design / Build and Refine. Each phase contains iterative steps to consider as you build your solution. The core of all of these has been discussed in previous chapters, this just helps bring them all together.

Discovery

The discovery phase is all about unearthing the real problem that needs solving and then understanding more about the people you are solving it for. It consists of three mains steps.

Define the Problem

I have written about this in the past. What a client *wants* and what they *need* are often very different things. The issue they bring to you may be a symptom of something else. You must dig and dig and dig until you can get to the actual problem that needs solving. This is a skill in itself, but remember to constantly ask **Why?**

Define the Users

Once you understand the problem, you must understand the people who are going to be involved and using the system. The client may have one idea, but the people on the ground using it may have a totally different one. User research is a very under-rated part of solution de-sign at times. You need to speak to them, run workshops with them and get to know them. Make the effort to understand them and you will be rewarded in heaven – or at least with positive feedback!

Define Success

What does winning look like for the client and for the users? Once you understand that, you need to decide what to record and measure to prove success (or disprove).

Design

Design the User Journey

Now, designing the User Journey does straddle the define and design phases a little. However. the key here is to understand and start to build the concept of the experiences for each of the five phases of the User Journey; Discover, On-board, Immerse, Master and Replay. You will revisit this during the design phase and you will add to it and probably take away from it – but it is an essential next step in the process.

Next, you are into the nuts and bolts of designing and building the experience. Initially, you will need to look at BMEM; Behaviour, Motivation, Emotion and Mechanics.

Behaviour

What is it you want your users to do? Some of this will have been addressed in the define phase, but now you need to go into a little more depth. What are the current behaviours and what do they need to be? Is there a large change needed?

Motivation

What motivates the people. Again, you will have covered some of this in the define phase, but now you must dive into it even further. Consider RAMP (relatedness, autonomy, mastery and purpose).

Also, don't forget rewards. A good balance of intrinsic and extrinsic rewards works very well!

Emotions

What do you want the users to *feel* when they engage with your gamified system? Should they experience fear, fun, love, humour, family, schadenfreude etc?

Mechanics

With everything else in place, you can start looking at the mechanics that will drive the system and engage your users. Will you need narratives, strategy, exploration or more?

Action / Feedback Loops

Discussed in the next section, Action / Feedback loops form the core of your gamified experience. Remember that they consist of a Call to Action, Action, Feedback and potentially a State Change.

Refine

All good design frameworks require you to iterate and refine your designs, this is no different. As you create new core loops and add new mechanics, you need to be flexible with your approach so that you can change and modify as you go. These days there is no such thing as a finished product!

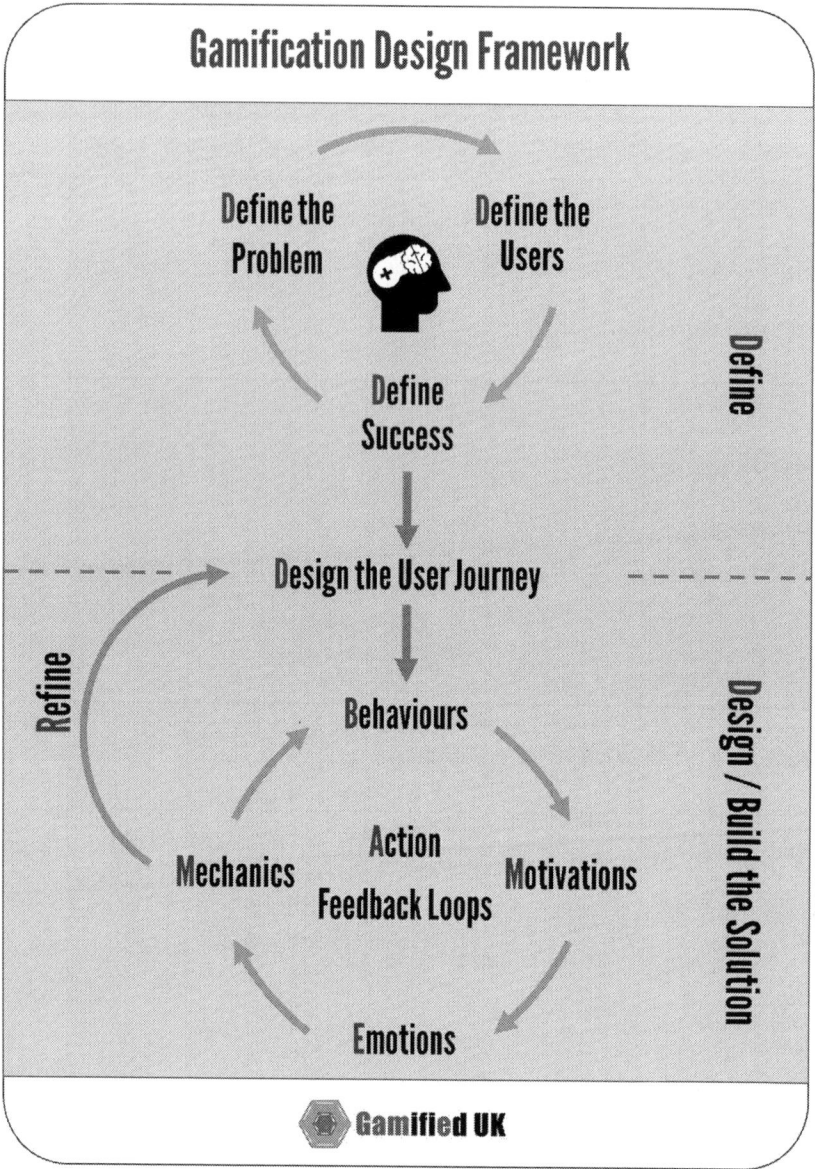

Figure 66 Gamification Design Framework in Full

How to Keep the User Engaged

I train hard, practicing the same activities repeatedly. It is how I improve. As my skills increase, I look for new challenges. My Master used to provide them, but I am beyond those now.

Action Feedback Loops

When we look at the user journey, there comes a point where the user will be "grinding". This term from games describes performing the same low skill, low-value activity repeatedly to increase your abilities, as we saw in the chapter on Flow. In our framework, this is the point where we move from *on-boarding* into *immersion*.

The basic concept is that the user performs an action or undertakes an activity successfully and something happens in the system. This may be a direct reward, an unlock, a change in the way the system behaves for them – anything that has a positive impact and encourages them to continue.

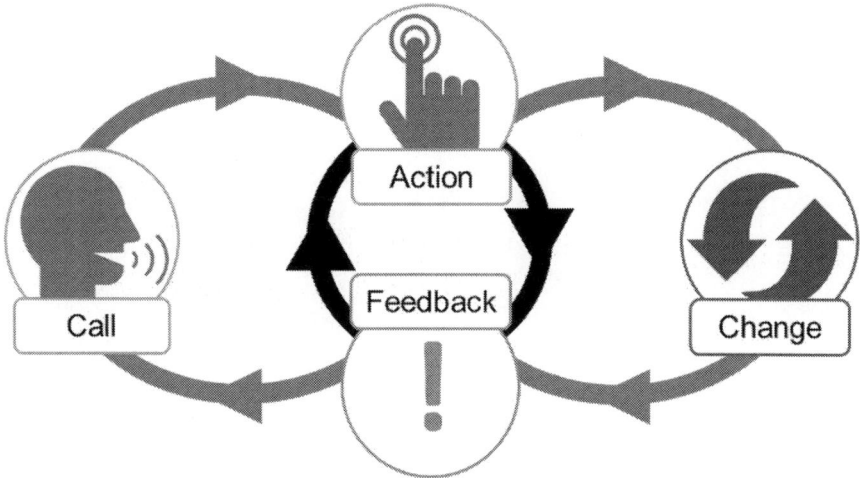

Figure 67 Action / Feedback Loops Example

Call to Action

The call to action is the instruction or prompt given to the user to do something. For example, a message on their phone to go for a walk.

User Action

This is the action the user then must take. In this case, go for a walk.

Feedback

Whilst the user is doing the action, they are provided with feedback. In our walk example, this may be encouragement to keep going or information about how far they have walked.

State Change

Eventually, something needs to change to keep the user engaged. This could be, in the case of our walker, an instruction to now walk further distances. In a game, this may be a difficulty increase. The state change then either leads to a new call to action or straight backing to the Action / Feedback loop.

I can feel the pent-up feelings of many people now who are about to scream the words *Operant Conditioning* at me.

For those who don't know, this was a form of behaviour modification that was made famous by BF Skinner [105]. He conducted experiments that rewarded or punished animals for types of behaviour.

Pull a lever; get a reward. Pull a lever; maybe get a reward. Push the wrong button; get a mild shock. He called this positive and negative reinforcement.

A big argument we have in gamification is that it is often viewed as a new and shiny form of operant conditioning. For the most part, this has seemed to be true in the past, especially in marketing implementations. Click; get a point. Click 10 times; get a badge etc. A big issue here is the lack of any kind of skill or effort needed to get the reward. Thankfully, there are many gamification experts out there doing their best to change that perception.

One of the concepts that I am trying to show with this activity loop example is the idea of having to earn access to new features by showing dedication and an increase in skills. Rating reviews or products is not difficult to do.

However, it introduces the user to the idea that if they want to do more, they can, *if* they are willing to put in the effort. Once the user unlocks the ability to add comments, they will then have to work hard and develop new skills to earn the next level of access.

When they are at the point where they can add their own reviews, they still must work hard, as they know others will now be rating and commenting on their work. However, with each increase in their level of access comes a sense of achievement, status, trust and more.

Again, if someone must earn a reward of some kind, it will be more important to him or her. Just giving people those rewards for activity that requires no level of skill or personal investment, is meaningless because they have not had to invest anything in getting it. Make them work for the rewards and they will value them a great deal more.

Action / Feedback *help* drive the user through a journey, but they do not *force* them. In the end, they must desire the end goal of the journey to put the effort in to get there. Gamification may just remove some of the friction from the journey, lowering barriers.

How to Balance a Gamified System

There is nothing worse than playing against people who are miles ahead of you in terms of either ability or equipment. It is very demoralising to lose time and time again when in reality, you never have a chance. My Master taught me that many times.

Balancing Gamified Systems

Take leaderboards as a good example. Very often the people at the top are always the same few names, repeatedly. For most companies, this does not seem to get addressed for some reason. It's a bit like pitting your local Sunday Dad's league against Chelsea every week. There is no opportunity for the Sunday players to ever be as good as Chelsea, they will get destroyed week after week until they give up playing. It is totally unfair and unbalanced. Therefore, in organised sports, you have divisions and leagues. You only play against people that you have a fair(ish) chance of beating.

Divisions

So, the first tip is if you find this happening, create leagues. Let the best of the best fight it out and let the others prove themselves against people they stand a chance with. If they get to top frequently, give them the opportunity to take on the next division and maybe get promoted. This has an added benefit of creating a pool of people you know are the best at something and (if you take into account the user journey) have become the masters. At this point, you should be trying to get them to give back, to train up those in the lower division.

Of course, this all relies on transparency and everyone understanding the rules. It is hard to get good at a game when you don't know the rules!

Handicaps

The second tip is to create balanced or relative scores, a bit like a golf handicap. A modifier can be applied to scores to either handicap those who are significantly better, or power up those who are newer or don't yet have all the required skills. So, for instance, the expert may get 50 points a day, whereas the lower skilled worker gets 30. However, because of the handicap modifier, you could have it set that every 1 point is worth 1.5 to the lower end player, giving them a slight boost (to 45 rather than 30) and helping push them a little higher in the tables. This does run the risk of better players screaming about it being unfair on them though.

Levels

You could also balance the game so that early on it is much easier to get points, so new players can quickly gain points, where hardened players need to work harder and demonstrate more skills to get the same number. This is a little like divisions as lower level players are more likely playing "against" other lower player levels, but their points can also begin to look like those of the higher-level players. This relies on keeping the "Flow" of challenge and skill well balanced. Always keeping a challenge, but never pushing the player too far out of their comfort zone or letting them get bored.

Team Balancing / Score Normalisation

Finally, team balancing. This is something I have come across a few times, especially in enterprise gamification. I have yet to find the perfect solution! The problem, the company wants departments to compete against each other, however, no department is the same size! So, what you can end up with is a team of 6 competing with a team of 30.

If your system is collecting points for various activities, it becomes very tough for the smaller team to compete with the larger team. To demonstrate the same activity, a team of 30 only needs 20% of their members to be active!

The first solution is to measure quality over quantity of activity. However, this still has the same issue. In a team of 30, you only need 20% to produce quality compared to 100% of the team of 6.

Another solution that I have considered but is complicated to really achieve well (I have tried, and it was ok in my tests) is creating normalised scores based on the average team size.

For example. If you have 4 teams of different sizes.

The average team size is calculated as 12. The score modifier for a team is calculated as your *team size / the average team size.*

Points are then multiplied by the modifier.

Team Size	Team Score	Modifier	Normalised Score
10	30	1.2	36
5	30	2.4	72
20	30	0.6	18
12	30	1	30
Average Team Size 12			

This requires great transparency and great communication of the rules to everyone, but it can work.

Learning from Games: Soda Crush

Candy Crush Saga from King games is one of the worlds most played games, boasting 93 million daily players at one point! I have always avoided it, but my wife has been into it for years. Finally, when she was explaining a level on the spin-off game Soda Saga, I cracked and downloaded it.

For those that don't know, Candy Crush and Soda Saga are a genre of puzzle game called "Match 3", first popularised by Bejewelled (though Shariki was the first example [106]). The basic concept sees you start with a board full of colourful tokens and you must swap two around that are next to each other to form rows of three. Create a row of three and they disappear, moving all the other tokens around.

King took this idea and turned the dial to 11! It's that turn of the dial that I want to speak about a bit. That is where they introduced what we would consider to be gamification in a game!

On-boarding

First, on-boarding is handled perfectly. The first few levels introduce you to the basic gameplay, simple images and animations explaining how the game works. Within minutes you feel totally at home playing. As the game progresses it shows you new features, as and when you need them – not before! Not sure what move to make? Wait a few seconds and the game will give you a hint!

Challenge and Skill

Every level is slightly harder than the last, perfectly balancing the challenge with the skill needed, never letting you drop into boredom. That is not to say you don't get frustrated. Some levels have you challenged for days, but they never make you feel that you can't do them – just that you need to try one more time to succeed!

As you progress, new challenges are added to the basic gameplay. Blocks that need to be destroyed, blocks that multiply, blocks that float, blocks that sink. Every few levels there is something new to discover.

Progress

From the outset, you can see what level you are on and what levels you can head towards. The map is nearly endless with hundreds and hundreds of levels!

Feedback

Feedback in Soda Saga is instant and plentiful! From satisfying animations and sounds as lines are made to bonus scores flashing up as you play to full-on, screen clearing explosions! After the level is finished you are shown your score, how well you did in the form of stars (3 being the best) and finally a leaderboard. In fact, the leaderboard is worth mentioning here.

When the leaderboard is shown at the end of a level, it shows you are the bottom of the table relative to your score. It then shows you rising up and displacing the person with the next lowest score at the top of the visible board. It never makes you feel like you didn't win or surpass your friends!

Friends

Soda Crush masterfully combines competition and a feeling of teamwork. For the most part, once connected to Facebook, you are competing with your friends. You always see who of your group has done best on a level. After that, you are shown your position relative to your friends on the leaderboards. However, there are also opportunities to feel like part of a team as certain challenges appear that require you to choose one of four to join.

The challenge may require you to score highly or destroy the most green sweets or create the most fish or any of a dozen other challenges! At the end of each level, your contribution is added to that of other members of the team. So even amid solo competition, you feel like you are part of something larger.

Help / Powerups

Soda Saga offers you aids as you play, from bonus special sweets to lollipop hammers and free swaps. When you feel like a level is just too hard, you can always use a few special items and powers to help push through. You can earn these specials powers by completing levels or by purchasing them with real money (of course).

There are also special sweets that can be created by combining more than 3 in a row, creating an extra level of strategy when considering what lines to create.

Reward Schedules

Soda Saga makes great use of reward schedules. Killing it by finishing levels without ever losing a life? There is a reward schedule for that! Coming back every day? There is a reward schedule for that! Soda Saga rewards both excellence and consistency.

Player Types

If I was to analyse what types in my HEXAD were catered for I would have to say everyone except for *Disruptors*.

- *Players* have plenty of points and leaderboards positions to play for.
- *Free Spirits* have a great deal of autonomy in how they play the game, there are multiple ways to win each map.
- *Achievers* have plenty of challenges to overcome and skills to learn.
- *Socialisers* get to see how their friends are doing, creating some friendly competition. On top of that, they get to feel like part of a team in certain challenges.
- *Philanthropists* are also catered for as they can donate lives to people in their networks.

All in all, Soda Saga is full to the brim with lessons for gamification designers. I have not even mentioned the micro narratives! Soda Saga once again proves that gamification designers should play games when they can. After all, our bread and butter is using lessons learned from games. You can't learn from them if you don't play them!

Rainbow Unicorn Was Here! 😊

Keeping it Simple

Simple things are easier to explain, understand, implement and maintain. Not everything needs to be complicated, just look at my Master...

Gamification, when you break it down, is usually used for one reason – to increase engagement with something. You may not have defined engagement as such, you may have spoken about active participation, or learning transfer, or productivity increase. However, they all point in one direction – to encourage people to do more of something or to do it better.

Some of the projects you have done or seen may have been long term focused, looking to increase intrinsic motivation of participants, others may have just been short term campaigns using simple mechanics to reward activity.

In my experience, gamification is mostly used as a way to boost interest in an activity and with that to increase any of the other factors that have been mentioned. Hand in hand with that there is often a level of education included, or on-boarding, to help elevate this to a new level.

If you consider activities needing interest and ability, like Flow, if a person is lacking interest, however motivated they may be via other factors, they will struggle to do things "happily". I like to think that gamification can be used to just nudge the needle on the interest side of the equation.

Sometimes that little nudge is all it takes to get an activity to happen, then you can work on other ways to get the activity to continue.

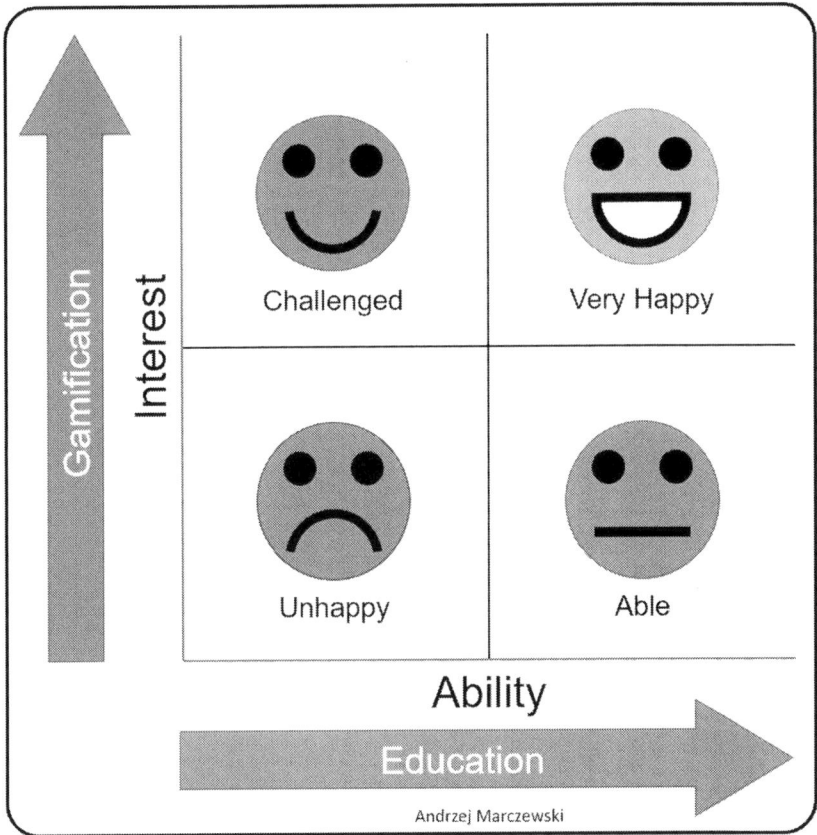

Figure 68 Interest vs Ability

Recently we had a challenge with my youngest daughter. We wanted her to eat a wider variety of vegetables. I created a chart and a simple narrative that had her eating vegetables to defeat various Batman villains. It used extrinsic rewards to encourage her to at least try certain vegetables.

In her mind, she lacked both interest and ability. The story line increased her interest so that it presented a challenge to her.

After trying carrots a few times, she was educated enough to know that she had the ability to eat them. Now, I am not saying she was in the "Very Happy" area of the chart because after finding she could eat them, her interest dropped as she realised she didn't like them much. However, at that point, she had eaten them in six successive meals and could no longer argue that she was unable to eat them!

You don't always have to create overly complicated plans. Sometimes you just need to make it all a bit more interesting!

Tying Loyalty into Gamification

Loyalty is important amongst ninjas, but it is not about rewards or bribes. For us it is a deep, emotional connection, relying on trust. Outside of the Ninja Monkey community, value, quality of service, trust and more are essential for fostering loyalty.

Some would do well to remember that.

True loyalty is like true love. It's irrational, hard to find & needs constant effort

A big focus in gamification these days is the concept of Loyalty. It is also an area of distinct misunderstanding if the typical loyalty programme examples are anything to go by!

Old School Loyalty

When we think of loyalty, especially when we consider it in the context of gamification, we tend to think of loyalty cards, air miles or other point collection systems. You spend £X amount and we will give you points that can go towards other goods or discounts.

When I was a kid, we used a petrol station called Texaco. There were two reasons for this. The first, it was on the way home from church on a Saturday evening and second, it was cheaper than other local options. Something they started to do was give you stickers based on how much petrol you bought. These stickers filled up cards, which could then be traded in against goods – the more cards you filled, the better the goods you could trade them in for. Using this method, my Mum and Dad managed to kit out our kitchen with new mugs, new glasses and I even got a Swiss Army Knife out of it!

All that makes it sound like we were loyal customers of Texaco. The truth of the matter really? It was convenient and cheap. The sticker scheme was a nice extra, but if we were not near home we would not go out of our way to find a Texaco garage for petrol, we would go where ever was close or cheap.

Real Consumer Loyalty

Loyalty in the consumer market is demonstrated when people will go out of their way to just use a particular product, service or brand. This is irrespective of convenience or price. For example, our Christmas Turkey.

Every year we buy our Christmas turkey from Graham Turner. He used to run a local butcher shop, just 15 minutes away. However, he changed the shop location to a new area, making his shop less convenient to get to. Even so, we still go there to get our turkey and any decent joints of meat we need. We have a butcher shop less than a 2-minute walk from us and we have two supermarkets less than a 5-minute drive from us. However, we always drive the 25 minutes to Graham. Why? Because he has cultivated loyalty in us. He and his staff make every visit feel special.

They treat us as old friends, greeting us by name or as Sir or Madam. The quality of their products is extremely high, and their customer service is unparalleled. Christmas Eve a few years ago, we got our Turkey and found out, once it was home, that it was not the size we had ordered. We called Graham to complain, he told us to come straight back and he would keep the shop open for us to sort out a replacement – Christmas Eve and he kept the shop open just for us. With service like this, I do not need to collect points to want to keep using Graham!

This kind of personal touch keeps people coming back time and time again, the feeling that you are special and important.

Big brands like Amazon know this as well, making every visit to the Amazon website a more personal experience. Algorithms are used to predict and recommend items that may be of interest to you, which are in my experience very accurate. You are greeted by name in a friendly manner. Emails you receive from them usually have relevance to you, offering tailor made, or seemingly tailor-made, deals that will interest you.

Tesco does the same, using their standard looking loyalty scheme to personalise the offers you get. Their website even states *"the more you use your Club-Card the better we can understand the sort of coupons you might like to receive"*. They are being honest; "keep using us and we will make sure the service you get will become more and more per-sonalised to what you want". It's the difference between getting a voucher for a DVD when you really need one for nappies.

Big brands like these can do this because they have huge amounts of data about you. You keep hearing about Big Data, well this is what it can offer the loyalty market – personalisation of everything. Amazon knows what I buy, so can tailor what I see. In 2013, they even patented a concept called "Anticipatory Shipping" [107].

The concept would see them delivering items even before you have ordered them – that's how well they feel they know your consumer habits! Tesco knows what I buy online and in-store because I scan my Club-Card after each shop and they can then identify me. It may sound creepy, but it begins to build a picture that allows these brands to make me feel like the centre of the experience.

Consumer loyalty is now about finding out who your customers are, what drives them and using that information to give them what they want and need in a timely, personalised and convenient manner.

Enterprise Loyalty

In the enterprise, loyalty is important as well, loyal employees are valuable. They work harder, and they are more likely to stay. However, many mistake loyalty for obligation or even lack of other options. A loyal employee is one who will stay even if they are offered a seemingly better opportunity; because they feel that they are valued and are valuable to the company they are with.

Some may stay because they feel some level of obligation or gratitude towards their employer for employing them though that will not last. Unless they feel valued, they will soon walk.

In much the same way as Graham Turner makes people feel they are at the centre of the experience when they are in his shop, employers need to make employees feel that they are at the centre of their experience in the company. If they feel like just another cog, they will feel no loyalty to the company at all.

Remember, feelings of obligation is not loyalty!

Four Loyalty Destinations

Barry Kirk of Maritz Motivation Solutions created a neat categorisation of loyalty. [108]

Inertia Loyalty: This is where people stay with something because it is too much effort to leave or change. Think of people in jobs just going through the motions. They may find it convenient to stay or too large a risk or effort to leave.

Mercenary Loyalty: Old school loyalty schemes fit here. Buy from us, collect points and get free stuff. My Consumer User Type sits here, and the Texaco stickers are a great example of this.

True Loyalty: This is where my loyalty to Graham Turner fits in. I go out of my way to use Graham's Butcher Shop because of the service, the quality and the experience. He may be more expensive and harder to get to, but that will not stop me! This is what you should be striving for.

Cult Loyalty: This is a strange one and one that cannot really be artificially created – it just happens. As Barry says, this is demonstrated by those who tattoo a brand logo to themselves or will only buy a Harley because that expresses deeply who they are. The closest I have seen to this kind of loyalty being manufactured is when Apple created the iPhone. Steve Jobs was often described as a cult leader with his "Reality Distortion Field".

The iPhone was a bit of leap of faith for Apple - it had to work. They started by making people feel that this was the future, to not have it would be to miss out on the future (Loss Aversion). Once people started to buy them, they made everyone else feel that if they did not have one, they were missing out and a loser (Social Pressure). This social pressure and sense of loss aversion has been continually cycling since the first iPhone was released.

It has kept people buying the iPhone even though it is considerably more expensive than any other phone on the market – and does considerably less than many other phones!

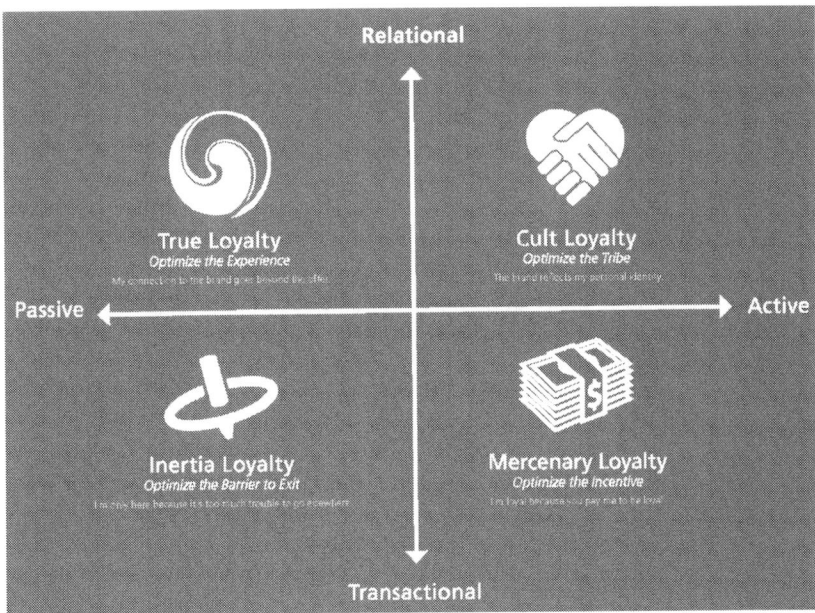

Figure 69 Barry Kirk's 4 Loyalty Destinations Framework

Creating loyalty is not easy, but a good place to start is to put the person whose loyalty you desire, back into the centre of the experience.

Make them feel that you as a brand, an employer or whatever else you may be, care about them directly and that you value them and understand them. Do not try to bribe them; loyalty must be earned.

Three States of Engagement and Loyalty

There are three basic states of Engagement and Loyalty: Not Engaged, Engaged and Loyal.

If you were running a shop, these three states would play out as:

- Will not shop with you for reason X, Y or Z.
- Will shop with you because of reason X, Y or Z.
- Will shop with you under any circumstance.

The question is, how do you convince people to shop with you and then how do you convince them to be loyal to you?

Getting Them Through the Door

The reason I use my local shop when I have to get something urgently is convenience. It may not be as good value as the supermarket, but it is easier for me walk to the shop – I am willing to pay extra for the convenience.

However, when I want my weekly shop, I will use the supermarket. There are two reasons for this. The first, it is much better value for that large a set of purchases. The second is that they deliver. Therefore, they make it easy for me to do and they make it a bit cheaper.

This gives us a small formula and a chart:

Chance of using Shop = Value × Convenience

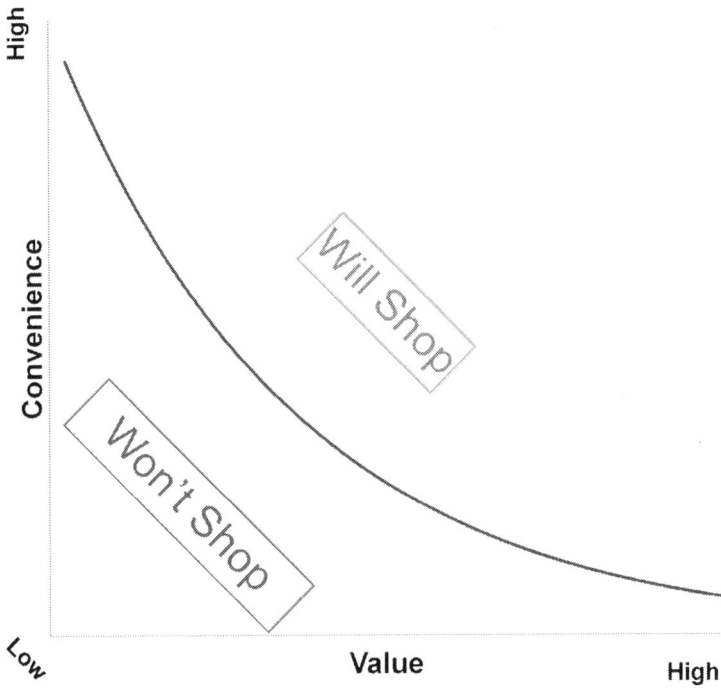

Figure 70 Basic Reason to Shop

We begin to get a picture of when a person will use your shop.

- Corner Shop: The convenience outweighs the value.
- Supermarket: The value outweighs convenience.
- Supermarket delivery: Value and convenience are both good, it is a no-brainer.

Now You Have Me, Keep Me!

That makes sense but does not tell us how to convert an engaged shopper into a loyal shopper. For that, we need something more – the magic sauce if you will. I mentioned that I would go to Graham Turner for my Christmas turkey every time.

There are two major reasons. First, the service that I receive when I go; they make the whole experience about me and I feel valued as a customer. The second is the quality of the product. It is less convenient than the supermarket and it is nowhere near the value of the supermarket, but I still use them. The service and the quality lower the barriers of value and convenience in my choice.

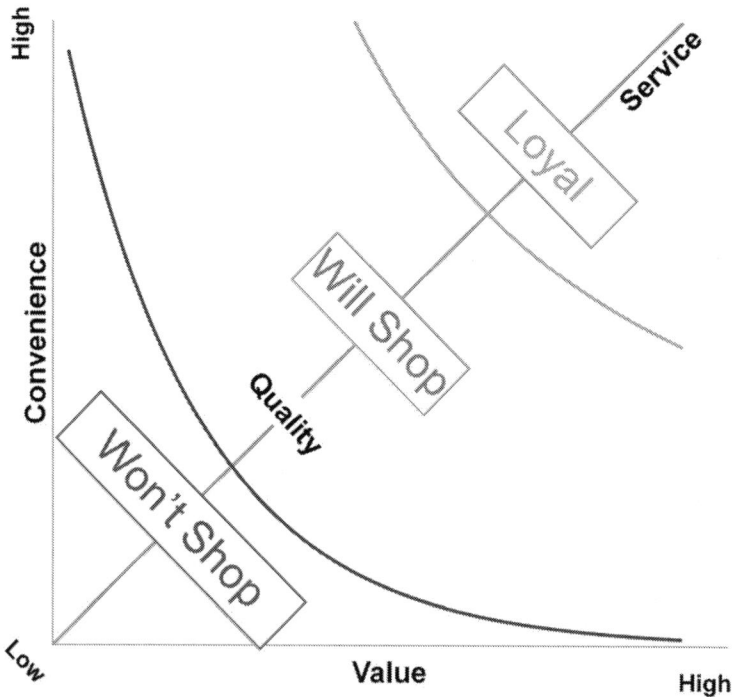

Figure 71 Quality and Service Creating Loyalty

The quality of the food from Turner's reduces the effect of convenience and value on my decision of where to shop. However, the service pushes into new territory.

The service is what makes me personally keep coming back, that is what keeps me loyal. The convenience and value become more a perception than a physical factor. I love the service; I love the quality, so the rest seems to be less of an issue to me.

If we put this into a formula, we get:

Loyalty = (Value × Convenience) × Quality × Service

How Is this of Use?

Of course, this is all simplified, but it does illustrate a few important considerations with loyalty. It is not good enough to be as good as or a bit better than your competition. You must be much better and way more valuable to people than your competition.

You must find what your unique selling point is and exploit it as much as possible.

This is not just applicable to shops; everything where you are trying to gain loyalty will work in a similar way. If you want people to keep coming back to your website, you need to find a unique reason why people will be loyal.

Many sites have a great design and quality writing. Maybe yours has advocacy and peer reviews that make it more trusted. That will get people to visit in the first place.

If that is the case, how about add something more, do weekly competitions, really drive down the effect other barriers have on people coming back.

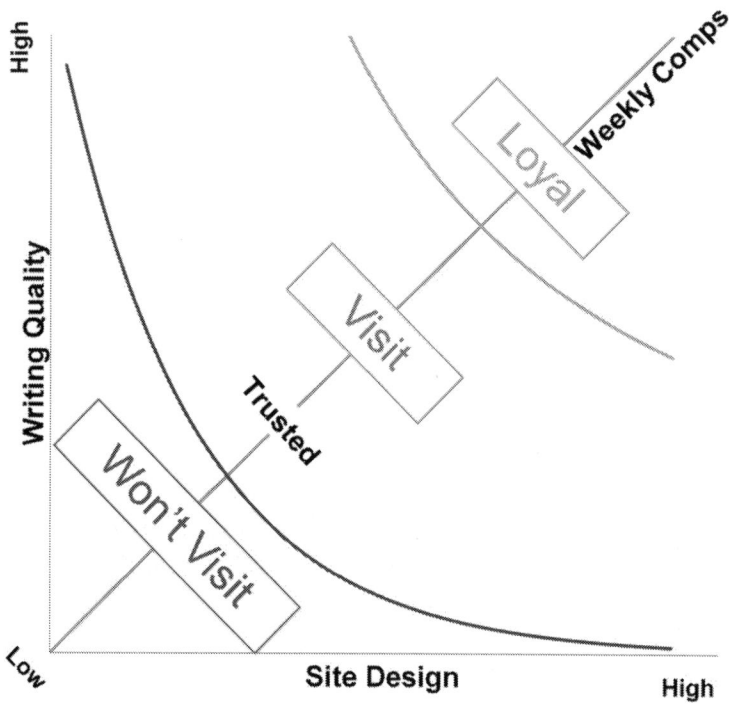

Figure 72 Example of Going Further

Every case is different. However, there are five basic actions you can take to cultivate this sort of loyalty:

1. Put the customer/user/employee at the centre of everything
2. Make them feel that they are getting value and that they are valued
3. Give them a reason to trust you and make them feel trusted
4. Give them quality service
5. Then start icing the cake with more features that people want and love.

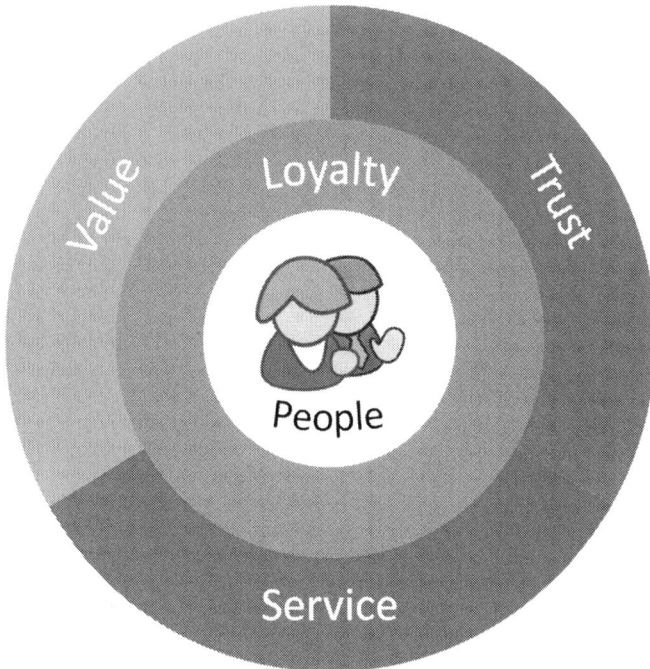

Figure 73 Key Components of Loyalty

Modelling Gamified Systems

I don't like spreadsheets, but they can be useful to a gamification designer when planning out point systems, reward paths and the like. I don't think they will help my *Master* when my plans come to fruition though.

An essential skill in gamification is being able to model a system and test out how your solution may flow. There are many ways to do this and people all have their favourite tools, but I wanted to share two of my "go-to" tools.

Spreadsheets

Yep – the least glamorous thing you can probably think of, but spreadsheets are my first port of call for modelling systems, especially if there is a points-based backbone to it.

With a spreadsheet, it is possible to automate a lot of the donkey work in trying to understand how points will be allocated and importantly, how long different types of users may take to achieve rewards and other goals. For example, the following image (Figure 74) shows a model of potential weekly usage for a highly engaged user over 12 weeks. The next image (Figure 75) shows the usage of a less engaged user.

You can see that the high engagement user will reach far more points over the 12-week period and average far more each week. Does this mean they will exhaust the system too quickly? Does it mean that users with lower engagement levels never have a hope of reaching certain levels?

	Pt	Week											
		1	2	3	4	5	6	7	8	9	10	11	12
Share on Twitter	5	2	1	3	1	4	1	1	1	2	1	1	1
Like on Facebook	5	2	2	2	1	3	1	4	1	4	1	1	1
Share on Facebook	10	4	5	1	6	1	2	1	1	1	2	2	2
Comment on Facebook	10	2	1	1	2	1	1	0	1	3	1	0	1
Rate on website	15	1	0	0	2	0	0	0	1	0	1	1	1
Weekly Score		95	75	45	120	55	40	35	45	70	55	45	55
Average Weekly Score		61											
Total for 10 Weeks		735											

Figure 74 Example of High Engagement

	Pt	Week											
		1	2	3	4	5	6	7	8	9	10	11	12
Share on Twitter	5	2	1	1	0	0	0	1	0	0	1	0	0
Like on Facebook	5	2	2	1	0	0	0	1	0	0	1	0	1
Share on Facebook	10	2	3	0	0	0	0	0	0	0	0	0	1
Comment on Facebook	10	1	0	0	0	0	0	0	1	0	1	0	1
Rate on website	15	2	1	0	0	0	0	0	0	0	0	0	0
Weekly Score		80	60	10	0	0	0	10	10	0	20	0	25
Average Weekly Score		18											
Total for 10 Weeks		215											

Figure 75 Example of Low Engagement

Another spreadsheet I use allows me to calculate what points to assign to certain activities and actions in a system based on the value to the user, the value to the system and the effort to the user. This way I can fine tune everything before users get their hands on it.

These kinds of models are in no way a replacement for user testing, but it is a way to get a step closer to usable before having to let people loose on your system!

Machinations

Machinations is a tool created by Joris Dorman's to help model game mechanics and feedback systems for game designers. It can be found at https://www.machinations.io/

As of 2018 it has had some great updates and should soon be able to run inside a browser rather than just as a standalone exe or flash file.

I won't go into detail about how to use it though, as there are already better explanations out there [109]. The interactive nature of the models can help you get an idea of how a system will work.

I have used it to model everything from basic points-based systems all the way up to resource management games.

A while back as an experiment, I created a very simple system that showed how a points, ranks and badges solution would work. This was then automated by Mikel Calvo and showed up an interesting concern with the system. After only about 8 days, a determined "player" could collect all the badges! Better to discover that in a simulation than 8 days after launching a £30,000 pilot!

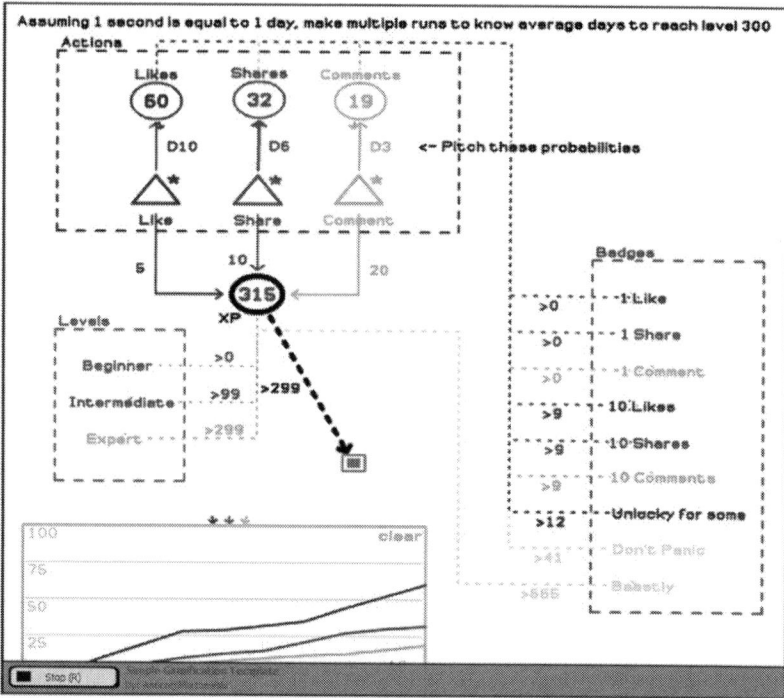

Figure 76 Machinations model of a simple gamified system

FINAL THOUGHTS

Five Steps to a Happier Life with Gamification

My master has his ups and downs, but over the years he has unknowingly used five key gamification lessons to lead a happier life. I wish to God he could user them to make my life happier.

Ok, this sounds a little "self helpy", but it came to me when I was doing a lecture for a group of master's students at Kings College. I ended the talk, rather by accident, with the following advice

> *"Always be sure you know why you are doing things, understand their purpose. It helps to then work towards small goals. That way no task, no matter how big – even the crushing student debt you probably have right now – will be manageable"*

Anyone who has seen me speak knows that I get quite passionate. What they may not know is that I react to the audience and adapt my talks accordingly. This group were great, and it felt right to give them a little ad-hoc advice. it got me thinking, though, what lessons from gamification am I applying in my own life day to day?

Goals, Purpose, Challenge, Feedback, Play

Goals

First and foremost – goal setting. I have spoken about goals in the past. Whatever method you wish to use, I personally feel that aiming at small manageable goals is the key. You must have an eye on the big picture, but that can be overwhelming. Break down everything to the smallest achievable goal you can.

For instance, you must build a website. This can be daunting if there are a lot of sections to create or specific interactivity. Rather than have that in mind, have the first smallest part in mind. What must happen. Well, you probably need to decide what languages to use. Easy. Next, what pages do you need? Simple and it goes on like that, incrementally increasing the difficulty of each task – consider it your user journey towards your main goal! Enrol, Engage, End Game!

Consider a game like Mario. You have your immediate goal – get to the other end of the map without dying. Then you have the level map that shows you other things you will have to do. Then you have your world map to show you everything that is going on. All the while you have an overriding goal – save the Princess.

Purpose

Next, you need to understand the purpose associated to each goal. I wrote about this recently, purpose whether it is meaningful or altruistic, is essential for happiness. Always ask the question "Why?" Why am I doing this? Why is this important? Then ask "What?" What is the benefit? What is the purpose? What's in it for me? For instance, when you must build that website you would create the following sentence. Why am I building this website? Why am I building this website and what is in it for me?

That answer may well be simple. You are building it because the client has asked you to and you get paid!

Again, it goes hand in hand with small goals and understanding where you are and what you are doing.

Again, back to Mario, you know the answers to both. Why am I running across this map and what will happen if I don't?

Because I need to save the Princess. If I don't, she dies!

Challenge

One of the things that keeps me happy is little challenges, usually, that don't relate to work. I always have them, whether it is creating a game, writing a book, learning something new etc. It breaks is one of the ways I force my mind to stop churning! I also love a statement from Andrea M. Kuszewski, that you can increase your intelligence by doing things the hard way [56]. Rather than use a prebuilt framework that does way more than you need, make it yourself! If you need to throw something in the bin – add an unnecessary obstacle like having to throw the paper across the room. After all, one of the definitions of what makes a game is from Bernard Suits *"the voluntary attempt to overcome unnecessary obstacles"*.

Feedback

Feedback is essential to any good system, even if it is your own internal system! You must know what success looks like and you must be able to measure it! This can be as simple as just getting a new bit of code to work and silently celebrating it, allowing yourself an extra bit of chocolate if you get an assignment finished early, buying that dress you saw because you lost the weight you had aimed for and so on.

Just remember to make sure that the reward fits the effort of the task/goal.

Play

This is the biggest and most important factor that keeps me sane and happy in my life – adding elements of play wherever I can. This can come in various forms. It may be that I stop and play with the kids for instance. It could be that I take a Batman break and do something playful for five minutes to reset my brain a little. I may just approach a new task with a more playful / lusory attitude and make the task more playful even if only in my own mind. Often play is more a state of mind.

There are many ways that games and gamification can help you in your day to day life, but these are just a few things that I do personally, so know they work!

Other Design Tips

These tips may well help you in your own designs; they are tried and tested by my Master. I have my own, but you will probably never get to see them.

Whilst there has been practical advice as we have gone along, there are a few more things that should be considered as you delve into designing your gamification solutions.

Getting to the Real Problem

It is simple to jump to *solutioneering* as soon as you feel you have a problem that needs fixing, creating the solution before you understand the problem. However, taking a step back and asking 4 simple questions can save you time and money in the long run.

- "What is the problem"
- "Why do we need to fix it"
- "What needs to change to fix it"
- "How do we do that"

What is the problem?

First, you need to explore What you are wanting to change. This is the easy bit and is likely to change, but it is a start. Be as specific as you can but be open minded as you explore further!

Most people already have this in mind when they first go to someone asking for gamification.

Why do we need to fix it?

Many gamification projects happen with the best of intentions, but are doomed to fail because no one stops to as the question "Why?"

315

Any behaviour focused intervention needs to have a clear focus, otherwise, you have no hope of solving your problems. You need to have a clear understanding of why you need to make a change. Is there an issue with people using a system? Are people not doing what you expected day to day. Are people not donating to your charity site when you thought they would?

Very often the answer to the initial what is "We want to improve engagement". However, that still begs the question "why?" Not just that, it also creates the new question "What is engagement?"

What needs to change to fix it?

To be successful you must identify what the root problems are, and what needs to change to fix them. If you have decided that people are not using your system because it is too complex, you must ask the question "what needs to change"

What may have looked like a behaviour issue, people were not using the system properly, may be a usability issue. That requires a totally different solution.

You will cycle between What and Why for a while until you have solid answers to the questions. You can also talk yourself in circles, so need to be pragmatic and occasionally start from scratch!

How do we do that?

Once you have got your solid answers to

- "What is the problem"
- "Why do we need to fix it"
- "What needs to change to fix it"

you can start to look at how to make those changes and gamification may form part of that. Then you can move onto the next phase.

Gamification Design Thinking

This is another process I make a lot of use of and is the base for my workshops. This is my interpretation of Design Thinking – a very well-known framework I have mixed it with a few well-known lenses for innovation – again, nothing new. It is presented here just as an aid for those who may not already be using it.

First, here is the basic process of design thinking.

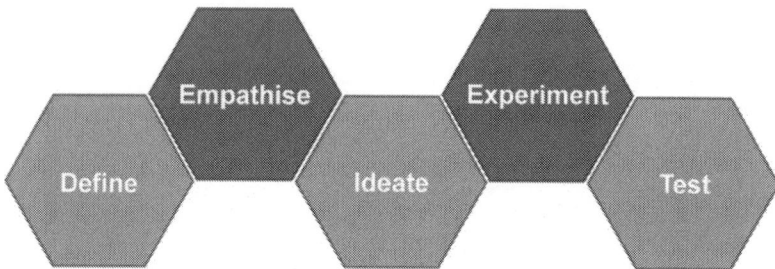

Figure 77 Gamification Design Thinking Outline

Define and understand the actual problem. Very often, the initial brief does not hold the problem that needs solving! Question, question and re-question and if needs be, re-frame the problem totally.

Empathise with the various people involved. Design thinking is all about putting the user first. So, consider what types of user you will have, this is not the same as User or Player Types; this is what people need from the system. Who are the users, why are they using the system? What does Mavis, 83 from Wales need, compared to Dave, 23 from Leeds?

Sometimes it is good to survey potential or current users to get an idea of whom they really are and then come up with some average users to role-play with!

Also, do not forget the stakeholders' needs in this. What do they want to achieve by gamifying the system? How will they react to it and your ideas?

Ideate – come up with ideas! Propose solutions and then analyse them (more in that in a moment). This is part of an iterative process, at this stage though there is no right answer.

Experiment with the best ideas. Pretotype, prototype, and do it again until you have something you think is worth taking forward.

Test your pretotype or prototype with the target audience and with the stakeholders. Iterate between testing and experimentation until you are ready to release at least a minimum viable product (MVP).

Whilst this is set out as a systematic process it is all iterative. At any point, you could go back to the start, but by the time you are into the experimentation phase, you should have a solid idea of where you are going.

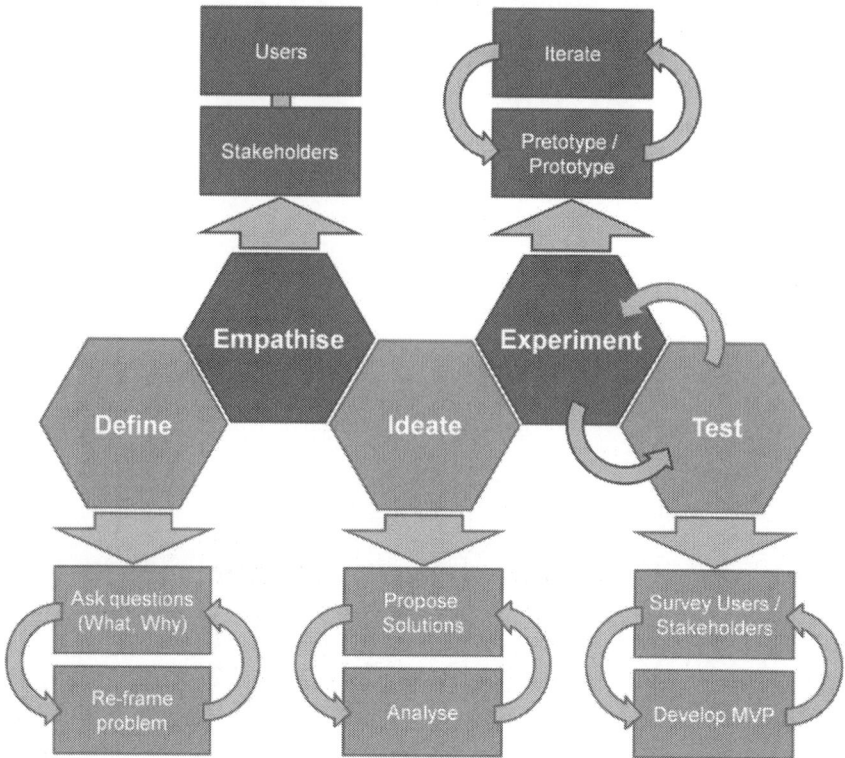

Figure 78 Gamification Design Thinking Expanded

Now, this is all great, but even high innovation must have a reality check from time to time. That being the case there are three common "lenses" that can be used to drive and balance innovation.

Innovation Lenses

Desirability: Is the product or solution you are looking at desirable to the users or the stakeholders? It may be great in your mind, but does it hit all the points they need?

Feasibility: Is your idea possible with current technology and skills? Can it really be done?

Viability: Can it be done within the constraints that reality often put upon us. Can it be done to budget and is it sustainable long term?

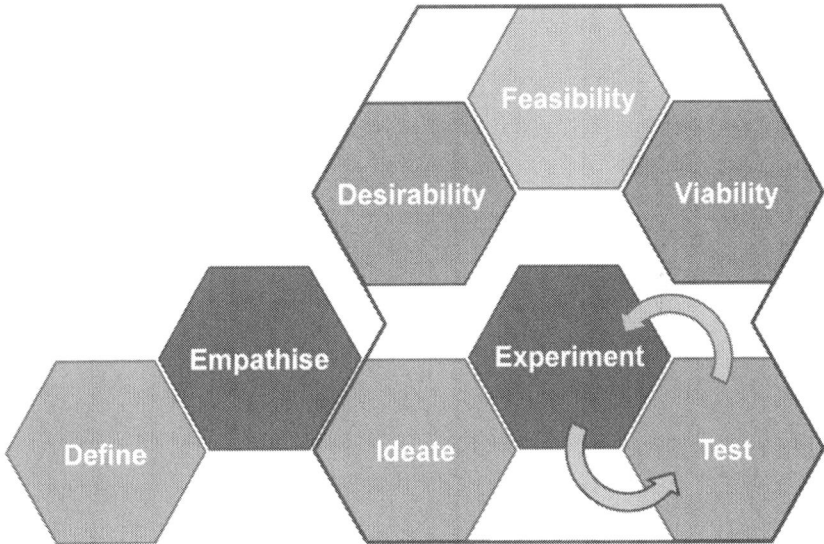

Figure 79 Innovation Lenses

Applying these lenses to the *Ideate, Experiment* and to a lesser extent, *Test* phases can save a lot of pain in the long term.

Really, by the time you are hitting the test phase, you should have a clear view of each lens!

Using this sort of process is very common in this day and age of constant innovation, but it can help focus your thoughts and designs, especially early on in your processes. Just as gamification should be, it all puts the user's experience first.

It Doesn't Have to Be Digital

It is easy to be left with the impression that gamification is all about digital or online creations. Whilst it is true that digital enables a great deal more flexibility and collaboration in systems, it is not the be all and end all!

There are many examples of analogue gamification, but here I share a simple system I use with my daughters.

The concept of reward charts is well known in parenting circles. You give your child stickers on a chart as they behave in the way they are meant to, or at least in the way you ask them to. It is a nice idea and can work, but as explained in the section about Overjustification effect, they can backfire if used for too long.

Once reward charts stopped working with my eldest daughter, I created a simple Behaviour Meter that is now stuck to our fridge. It has a scale of 0 to 10 and that's it.

Figure 80 Simple analogue example of gamification

Throughout the day, my wife and I alter the position of the arrow depending on how my daughter is behaving. We don't tell her what the current reading is – she must look at the feedback for herself. Of course, this is on top of other verbal feedback we are giving her as well. However, this gives her a fixed reminder of how we feel she is doing.

There are no rewards attached to her rating on the chart, it is just there as a way of giving her relevant feedback. After about a year of using the chart, my daughter added a second arrow. The second arrow represents where she feels her behaviour is on the scale. If there is a difference, we discuss why and what needs to be done to close the gap. It is very simple, but as with a lot of gamification, just giving feedback can solve many issues.

I mentioned earlier a similar example I created to get my youngest daughter to eat more vegetables! Looking more like the traditional reward chart, this focused on a story. Over the summer holiday she had to defeat some of Batgirl's greatest foes, by eating certain vegetables. Each bad guy had a vegetable associated to them. She could choose who she was fighting that day and had to eat a portion of that vegetable. Once she had eaten the specified amount, she got a small reward and defeated that bad guy. Once she had defeated all the bad guys, she got to take on the Joker by eating a meal with at least three of the vegetables on her plate.

The End

That's pretty much it. My sympathies if you have read this far, especially if you already had the first edition! This is where we shall part ways. My *Master* has nothing left for me, so read these last pieces of advice and start creating.

I have my own work to finish.

Just as all good stories must have a beginning, they must also have an end. I hope this book has given you enough of an insight into the many faceted worlds of gamification to be able to start making use of it in your own projects.

I wanted to leave you with a few last tips and things to think about.

The first is **don't be bogged down by definitions**. I spent time at the beginning of the book explaining Game Thinking and why I feel it is helpful; however, the reality is we will never fully agree on the answer to the question "What is gamification?" A better question is "Does this solve the problem", or "Is this the best solution for the users?" It doesn't matter if you use gamification, games or Ninja Monkeys.

As a gamifier, **you are a problem solver**. Your job is to solve an issue the client is having. The likelihood is you will favour a solution with a game like flavour – but I would hope that you would not reject a solution just because it is not what you would consider "proper" gamification.

Never reject an idea that may be better than yours, just because you don't know how to execute it. If the answer is to create a game, it doesn't matter if you think that is true gamification – it is still the answer and you should do what you can to facilitate it!

Finally, I will leave you with my seven essential tips for gamification glory!

1 Ensure that gamification adds **benefit** and **value** to all.

Define clear, measurable **goals** and provide feedback on **progress** towards them. **2**

3 **Intrinsic** motivation leads to longer term & quality **engagement**.

Be open about what data is collected and why. **Trust** is essential. **4**

5 **Extrinsic** rewards can engage over short periods like **onboarding / enrol**.

Define, collect and **act** upon appropriate metrics. **6**

7 Be flexible and **adapt** as user needs and behaviours change.

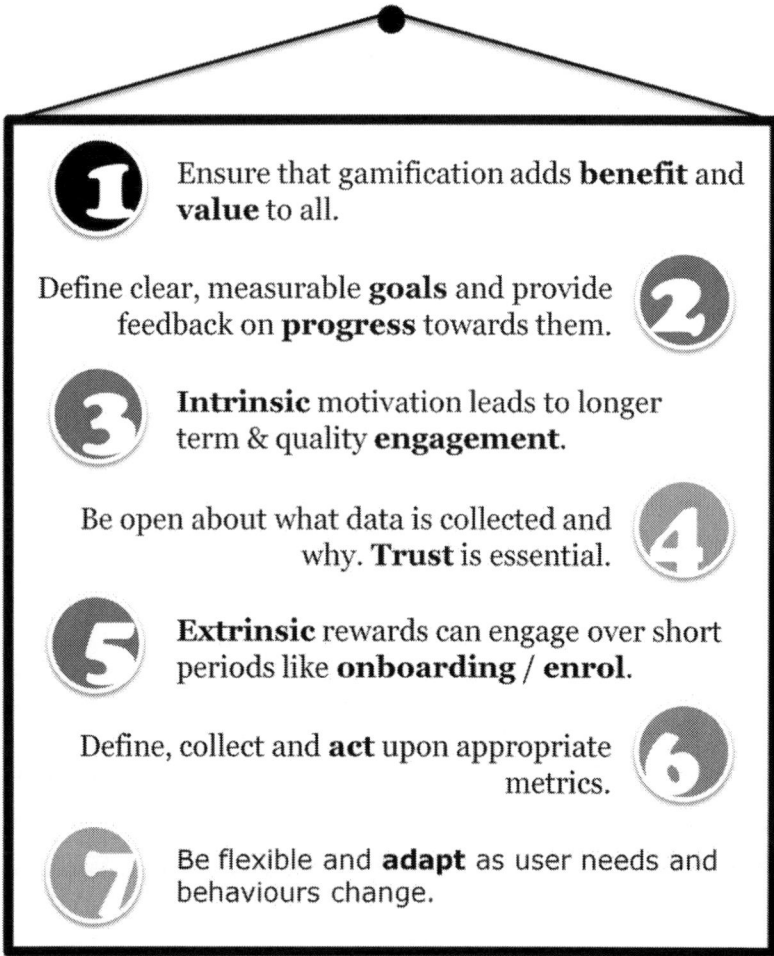

Figure 81 7 Top Tips

THE END

GLOSSARY

Autonomy: Freedom/agency to act as you wish.

Engagement: Active, focused and intrinsically motivated participation.

Extrinsic Reward: Something that is external, such as monetary rewards for doing something.

Fiero: An Italian word that is used in gamification to describe a sense of great achievement or triumph over adversity – the sort that has you fist pumping in the air!

Flow: A concept described by Mihaly Csikszentmihalyi. In gamification, we talk about it as a place between boredom and frustration where the skills of the player match the level of challenge. They lose all sense of self and time seems to go by much faster.

Game Aesthetics: The experience of the end user.

Game Dynamics: Emergent activities of the users as they interact with mechanics.

Game Elements/Components: These are bits that are taken from games, such as progress bars, missions, points, badges etc.

Game Mechanics: Explicit sets of rules that define the outcomes of user activities.

Game Thinking: The use of games and game-like approaches to solve problems and create better experiences.

Gamification: The use of game thinking to create more game-like experiences.

Intrinsic motivation: Personal/internal reasons to do something. Relatedness, Autonomy, Mastery and Purpose are examples of this.

Loyalty: Allegiance to something, for example, a brand, that goes beyond normal interest. People loyal to a brand will go out of their way, ignoring value and convenience to own products from that brand.

Mastery: Achieving something such as learning a new skill.

Naches: A Yiddish word that means "feeling of pride at the achievement of your children". In gamification, we use this word to describe the feeling people get when people achieve something thanks to the help they have given them.

On-boarding: Refers to the first steps taken in a new system, for example, an interactive tutorial.

Overjustification Effect: The decrease of intrinsic motivation to perform a task or tasks when an extrinsic reward is introduced, and the reward becomes more important than the original task.

Player: Also called the user, the target person who will be using the gamified system.

Player Journey: Defined in this book as four or five phases that the user goes through whilst using a system, Discovery, On-boarding, Immersion, Mastery and Replay

Purpose: three variations.

1. A sense of direction, such as goals or story-lines/narratives.
2. Epic Meaning: the feeling that you are involved in something with greater meaning or purpose.
3. Altruism (selfless acts for the benefit of others).

Relatedness: Social connection to others.

Serious Game: A real game that is built primarily for purposes other than pure entertainment.

Underjustification Effect: The decrease in motivation to perform a task or tasks when supposedly motivational techniques are applied in place of perceived air compensation or treatment.

REFERENCES

1. Starship Troopers: Battlespace - Starship Troopers Wiki - Roughnecks Chronicles. Available at: http://starshiptroopers.wikia.com/wiki/Starship_Troopers:_Battlespace. (Accessed: 28th June 2015)

2. Marczewski, A. Yet Another Review Site - Games News and Reviews. Available at: http://www.yetanotherreviewsite.co.uk/. (Accessed: 28th June 2015)

3. Marczewski, A. *Gamification: A Simple Introduction & a Bit More [Kindle Edition]*. (2012).

4. Pelling, N. The (short) prehistory of "gamification"... | Funding Startups (& other impossibilities) on WordPress.com. (2011). Available at: https://nanodome.wordpress.com/2011/08/09/the-short-prehistory-of-gamification/. (Accessed: 28th June 2015)

5. Marczewski, A. A look at Wikipedia's definition of Gamification over the years. (2014).

6. Deterding, S., Dixon, D., Khaled, R. & Nacke, L. From Game Design Elements to Gamefulness : Defining " Gamification ". in *Envisioning Future Media Environments* 9–11 (2011). doi:10.1145/2181037.2181040

7. Werbach, K. (Re)defining gamification: A process approach. in *Lecture Notes in Computer Science (including subseries Lecture Notes in Artificial Intelligence and Lecture Notes in Bioinformatics)* **8462 LNCS,** 266–272 (Springer Verlag, 2014).

8. Huizinga, J. *Homo Ludens: A study of the play -- element in culture. a study of the element of play in culture* (1950). doi:10.1177/090756820200900400

9. Ludic - definition of ludic in English from the Oxford dictionary. *Oxford Dictionaries* Available at: http://www.oxforddictionaries.com/definition/english/ludic. (Accessed: 5th September 2015)

10. Parlett, D. What's a ludeme? Available at: http://www.davidparlett.co.uk/gamester/ludemes.html. (Accessed: 4th July 2015)

11. Bateson, G. A Theory of Play and Fantasy. in *Steps to an Ecology of Mind* 177–193 (1972). doi:10.1016/0732-118X(91)90042-K

12. Goffman, E. Frame Analysis: An Essay on the Organization of Experience. *Contemporary Sociology* **10,** 60 (1981).

13. Hirsh-Pasek, K. & Golinkoff, R. M. Why play= learning. *Encycl. Early Child.* 1–7 (2008).

14. Crawford, C. *Chris Crawford on Game Design. Computer* **2006,** (2003).

15. Minsky, M. Jokes and the Cognitive Unconscious. in *Cognitive Constraints on Communication - Representations* (eds. Vaina, L. & Hintikka, J.) 175–200 (Reidel, Boston, 1984).

16. Suits, B. *The Grasshopper: Games, Life and Utopia.* (Toronto: University of Toronto Pres, 2005).

17. Rollings, A. & Morris, D. *Game Architecture and Design. Education* (1999).

18. Schell, J. *The Art of Game Design: A book of lenses.* (Morgan Kauffmann, 2008).

19. Salen, K. & Zimmerman, E. *Rules of Play: Fundamentals of Game Design. Leonardo* **37,** (2004).

20. Sutton-Smith, B. The opposite of play is not work — it is depression. *Stanford Neurosciences Institute* (2015). Available at: https://neuroscience.stanford.edu/news/opposite-play-not-work-—-it-depression. (Accessed: 16th January 2017)

21. Hunicke, R., LeBlanc, M. & Zubek, R. MDA: A Formal Approach to Game Design and Game Research. *Work. Challenges Game AI* 1–4 (2004). doi:10.1.1.79.4561

22. Fun - definition of fun in English from the Oxford dictionary. Available at: http://www.oxforddictionaries.com/definition/english/fun. (Accessed: 8th July 2015)

23. LeBlanc, M. 8 Kinds of Fun. Available at: http://8kindsoffun.com/. (Accessed: 8th July 2015)

24. Vargas, J. A. In 'Darfur Is Dying,' The Game That's Anything But. *The Washington Post* Available at: http://www.washingtonpost.com/wp-dyn/content/article/2006/04/30/AR2006043001060.html. (Accessed: 29th June 2015)

25. Peckham, M. Foldit Gamers Solve AIDS Puzzle That Baffled Scientists for a Decade. *TIME Magazine* (2011). Available at: http://techland.time.com/2011/09/19/foldit-gamers-solve-aids-puzzle-that-baffled-scientists-for-decade/. (Accessed: 3rd August 2015)

26. Lazzaro, N. Tilt World: Plant Trees. Available at: http://www.tiltworld.com/planttrees.html. (Accessed: 3rd August 2015)

27. Play to Cure: Genes in Space | Cancer Research UK. Available at: http://www.cancerresearchuk.org/support-us/play-to-cure-genes-in-space. (Accessed: 3rd August 2015)

28. Kapp, K. Two Types of Gamification « Karl Kapp. Available at: http://karlkapp.com/two-types-of-gamification/. (Accessed: 29th June 2015)

29. Caffrey, M. Toward a History Based Doctrine for Wargaming. *Military Book Reviews* (2000). Available at: http://www.strategypage.com/articles/default.asp?target=WARGHIS2.htm&reader=long. (Accessed: 14th April 2016)

30. Fashion & Mash | Selfridges introduces Elfridges gaming app for Holiday 2014. *Fashion & Mash* Available at: http://fashionandmash.com/2014/12/10/selfridges-introduces-elfridges-gaming-app/. (Accessed: 3rd August 2015)

31. Schell, J. Jesse Schell: When games invade real life (video TEDx). *TED [online]* (2010). Available at: http://www.ted.com/talks/jesse_schell_when_games_invade_real_life.html.

32. Paul, B. R. & Elder, L. Minature Guide to Ethical Reasoning. *Found. Crit. Think.* 1–45 (2003).

33. News, C. H. B. & Beijing. China 'social credit': Beijing sets up huge system. *BBC News* online (2015).

34. Marczewski, A. Pokemon Go: The Good, The Bad and Some Lessons. (2016).

35. Marczewski, A. & Andrzej. The ethics of gamification. *XRDS Crossroads, ACM Mag. Students* **24,** 56–59 (2017).

36. Maslow, a. A theory of human motivation. *Readings Manag. Psychol.* 20–35 (1989).

37. Tay, L. & Diener, E. Needs and subjective well-being around the world. *J. Pers. Soc. Psychol.* **101,** 354–365 (2011).

38. Werbach, K. & Hunter, D. *For the Win: How Game Thinking Can Revolutionize Your Business.* (Wharton Digital Press, 2012).

39. Ryan, R. M. & Deci, E. L. Intrinsic and Extrinsic Motivations: Classic Definitions and New Directions. *Contemp. Educ. Psychol.* **25,** 54–67 (2000).

40. Ryan, R. M. & Deci, E. L. Self-determination theory and the facilitation of intrinsic motivation, social development, and well-being. *Am. Psychol.* **55,** 68–78 (2000).

41. Pink, D. H. *Drive: The surprising truth about what motivates us. Distribution* (Canongate, 2009). doi:10.1002/casp

42. Sigmund, K. & Hauert, C. Altruism. *Current Biology* **12,** R270–R272 (2002).

43. Grant, A. M. The significance of task significance: Job performance effects, relational mechanisms, and boundary conditions. *J. Appl. Psychol.* **93,** 108–124 (2008).

44. Glott, R., Schmidt, P. & Ghosh, R. *Wikipedia Survey – Overview of Results. United Nations University MERIT* (2010).

45. Harbaugh, W. T., Mayr, U. & Burghart, D. R. Neural responses to taxation and voluntary giving reveal motives for charitable donations. *Science* **316,** 1622–1625 (2007).

46. Csikszentmihalyi, M. *Flow: The psychology of optimal performance. Optimal experience: Psychological studies of flow in consciousness* (1990).

47. Kim, A. J. Beyond Player Types: Kim's Social Action Matrix. Available at: http://amyjokim.com/blog/2014/02/28/beyond-player-types-kims-social-action-matrix/. (Accessed: 15th September 2015)

48. Bateman, C. BrainHex. Available at: http://blog.brainhex.com/. (Accessed: 15th September 2015)

49. Bartle, R. A. Hearts, clubs, diamonds, spades: Players who suit MUDs. *J. MUD Res.* **1,** 19 (1996).

50. Herbert, B., Charles, D., Moore, A. & Charles, T. An Investigation of Gamification Typologies for Enhancing Learner Motivation. in *2014 International Conference on Interactive Technologies and Games* 71–78 (IEEE, 2014). doi:10.1109/iTAG.2014.17

51. Hof, R. Second Life's First Millionaire - BusinessWeek. *Business Week* (2006). Available at: http://www.businessweek.com/the_thread/techbeat/archives/2006/11/second_lifes_fi.html. (Accessed: 10th July 2015)

52. Paulhus, D. L. Toward a Taxonomy of NGOs. *Association of Phsychological Science* (2014).

53. Schwarz, N. Cognitive aspects of survey methodology. *Applied Cognitive Psychology* **21**, 277–287 (2007).

54. Salamone, J. D. & Correa, M. The Mysterious Motivational Functions of Mesolimbic Dopamine. *Neuron* **76**, 470–485 (2012).

55. Puig, M. V. & Miller, E. K. The Role of Prefrontal Dopamine D1 Receptors in the Neural Mechanisms of Associative Learning. *Neuron* **74**, 874–886 (2012).

56. Kuszewski, a. You can increase your intelligence: 5 ways to maximize your cognitive potential : Scientific American. *Scientific American Blog* 1–8 (2011). Available at: http://www.scientificamerican.com/blog/post.cfm?id=you-can-increase-your-intelligence-2011-03-07&WT.mc_id=SA_WR_20110309%5Cnpapers2://publicati on/uuid/8B01D224-0BBB-47A9-A6F6-D06010E63DEB. (Accessed: 22nd March 2015)

57. Kuszewski, A. The Science Of Pleasure: Part III- The Neurological Orgasm. *Science 20* (2010). Available at: http://www.science20.com/rogue_neuron/science_pleasure _part_iii_neurological_orgasm. (Accessed: 22nd March 2015)

58. Zak, P. J. The Top 10 Ways to Boost Good Feelings. *Psychology Today* (2013). Available at: https://www.psychologytoday.com/blog/the-moral-molecule/201311/the-top-10-ways-boost-good-feelings. (Accessed: 22nd March 2015)

59. Kosfeld, M., Heinrichs, M., Zak, P. J., Fischbacher, U. & Fehr, E. Oxytocin increases trust in humans. *Nature* **435**, 673–6 (2005).

60. Concordia University. 'Love hormone' oxytocin carries unexpected side effect -- ScienceDaily. *Science Daily* (2014). Available at: http://www.sciencedaily.com/releases/2014/01/14012211262 6.htm. (Accessed: 22nd March 2015)

61.	Association for Psychological Science. The Dark Side of Oxytocin - Association for Psychological Science. (2013). Available at: http://www.psychologicalscience.org/index.php/news/releases/the-dark-side-of-oxytocin.html. (Accessed: 22nd March 2015)

62.	Weldone, M. Your Brain on Story: Why Narratives Win Our Hearts and Minds. *Pacific Stand.* (2014).

63.	Weldon, M. Your Brain on Story: Why Narratives Win Our Hearts and Minds. *Pacific Standard* (2014). Available at: http://www.psmag.com/books-and-culture/pulitzer-prizes-journalism-reporting-your-brain-on-story-why-narratives-win-our-hearts-and-minds-79824. (Accessed: 22nd March 2015)

64.	Nguyen, T. Hacking Into Your Happy Chemicals: Dopamine, Serotonin, Endorphins and Oxytocin. *The Utopian Life* (2014). Available at: http://www.huffingtonpost.com/thai-nguyen/hacking-into-your-happy-c_b_6007660.html. (Accessed: 22nd March 2015)

65.	Lee, K. Games and Your Brain: How to Use Gamification to Stop Procrastinating. *The Buffer Blog* (2013). Available at: https://blog.bufferapp.com/brain-playing-games-why-our-brains-are-so-attracted-to-playing-games-the-science-of-gamification. (Accessed: 22nd March 2015)

66.	Zanettini, C. Effects of endocannabinoid system modulation on cognitive and emotional behavior. *Frontiers in Behavioral Neuroscience* **5,** (2011).

67.	Kim, A. J. The Player's Journey: Designing Over Time. Available at: http://amyjokim.com/2012/09/14/the-players-journey-designing-over-time/. (Accessed: 13th March 2015)

68. Herger, M. Gamification and Law or How to stay out of Prison despite Gamification. (2012). Available at: http://enterprise-gamification.com/index.php?option=com_content&view=article&id=65:gamification-and-law-or-how-to-stay-out-of-prison-despite-gamification&catid=4:blog&Itemid=251&lang=en. (Accessed: 9th July 2015)

69. giffgaff Case Study. Available at: http://www.figarodigital.co.uk/case-study/giffgaff.aspx. (Accessed: 10th July 2015)

70. Keeler, A. Gamify Your PD: Badges and Level Up. (2014).

71. Lindqvist, J., Cranshaw, J., Wiese, J., Hong, J. & Zimmerman, J. I'm the Mayor of My House: Examining Why People Use foursquare - a Social-Driven Location Sharing Application. in *CHI '11 Proceedings of the 2011 annual conference on Human factors in computing systems* **54,** 2409–2418 (2011).

72. Lepper, M. R., Greene, D. & Nisbett, R. E. Undermining children's intrinsic interest with extrinsic reward: A test of the 'overjustification' hypothesis. *J. Pers. Soc. Psychol.* **28,** 129–137 (1973).

73. Mekler, E. D. Gamification Considered Harmful? | Gamification Research Network. (2014). Available at: http://gamification-research.org/2014/08/gamification-considered-harmful/. (Accessed: 16th September 2015)

74. Kapp, K. *The Gamification of Learning and Instruction: Game-based Methods and Strategies for Training and Education.* (Pfeiffer & Company, 2012).

75. Deci, E. L., Betley, G., Kahle, J., Abrams, L. & Porac, J. When Trying to Win. *Personal. Soc. Psychol. Bull.* **7,** 79–83 (1981).

76. Niederle, M. & Vesterlund, L. Gender differences in competition. *Negot. J.* **24,** 447–463 (2008).

77. Bryant, B. K. The Effects of the Interpersonal Context of Evaluation on Self- and Other-Enhancement Behavior. *Child Dev.* **48,** 885–892 (1977).

78. SCHAFFER, N. 13 Expert Views on Klout's New Scoring Algorithm. (2012). Available at: http://maximizesocialbusiness.com/klout-experts-social-influence-algorithm-7024/. (Accessed: 9th July 2015)

79. Bühren, C. & Pleßner, M. The Trophy Effect. *Journal of Behavioral Decision Making* (2013). doi:10.1002/bdm.1812

80. Thaler, R. H. Toward a positive theory of consumer choice. *J. Econ. Behav. Organ.* **1,** 39–60 (1980).

81. Antin, J. & Churchill, E. F. Badges in social media: A social psychological perspective. *Chi 2011* 1–4 (2011).

82. Woolley, K. & Fishbach, A. Immediate Rewards Predict Adherence to Long-term Goals. *Personal. Soc. Psychol. Bull.* **43,** 151–162 (2017).

83. Fishbach, A. & Choi, J. When thinking about goals undermines goal pursuit. *Organ. Behav. Hum. Decis. Process.* **118,** 99–107 (2012).

84. Williams, H. L., Conway, M. A. & Cohen, G. Autobiographical Memory. *Memory in the Real World* 424 (2007). doi:10.1017/CBO9780511558313

85. Trope, Y. & Liberman, N. Construal-level theory of psychological distance. *Psychol. Rev.* **117,** 440–463 (2010).

86. Doran, G. T. There's a S.M.A.R.T. way to write managements's goals and objectives. *Manage. Rev.* **70,** 35 (1981).

87. UnMetric. Engagement Score Revised. Available at: https://unmetric.com/engagement/.

88. Koster, R. *Theory of Fun for Game Design. A Theory of Fun for Game Design* (2005).

89. Mischel, W., Ebbesen, E. B. & Zeiss, A. R. Cognitive and attentional mechanisms in delay of gratification. *J. Pers. Soc. Psychol.* **21,** 204–218 (1972).

90.   Casey, B. J. *et al.* Behavioral and neural correlates of delay of gratification 40 years later. *Proc. Natl. Acad. Sci. U. S. A.* **108,** 14998–15003 (2011).

91.   Kidd, C., Palmeri, H. & Aslin, R. N. Rational snacking: Young children's decision-making on the marshmallow task is moderated by beliefs about environmental reliability. *Cognition* **126,** 109–114 (2013).

92.   Fsa. The Turner Review A regulatory response to the global banking crisis. *Fsa* (2009). Available at: http://www.fsa.gov.uk/pubs/other/turner_review.pdf. (Accessed: 17th July 2015)

93.   Deci, E. L., Koestner, R. & Ryan, R. M. A meta-analytic review of experiments examining the effects of extrinsic rewards on intrinsic motivation. *Psychol. Bull.* **125,** 627-668; discussion 692-700 (1999).

94.   Robson, K., Plangger, K., Kietzmann, J. H., McCarthy, I. & Pitt, L. Is it all a game? Understanding the principles of gamification. *Bus. Horiz.* **58,** 411–420 (2015).

95.   Aristotle. *Aristotle On the Soul.* (350AD).

96.   Izard, C. E., Libero, D. Z., Putnam, P. & Haynes, O. M. Stability of emotion experiences and their relations to traits of personality. *J. Pers. Soc. Psychol.* **64,** 847–860 (1993).

97.   Ekman, P. An argument for basic emotions. *Cogn. Emot.* **6,** 169–200 (1992).

98.   Nathanson, D. L. *Shame and pride : affect, sex, and the birth of the self.* (Norton, 1992).

99.   Robinson, D. L. Brain function, emotional experience and personality. *Neth. J. Psychol.* **64,** 152–168 (2008).

100.   Luomala, K. & Campbell, J. The Hero with a Thousand Faces. *J. Am. Folk.* **63,** 121 (1950).

101. Comberg, D. Kurt Vonnegut on the Shapes of Stories. *YouTube* (2010). Available at: https://www.youtube.com/watch?v=oP3c1h8v2ZQ. (Accessed: 29th May 2017)

102. Goldberg, L. *Russian literature in the nineteenth century : essays.* (Magnes Press Hebrew University, 1976).

103. Mediratta, B. & Bick, J. The google way: Give engineers room. *New York Times, October* 21–22 (2007).

104. Bartle, R. A. How to cheat at mMos. (2012).

105. Skinner, B. F. Operant behavior. *American Psychologist* **18,** 503–515 (1963).

106. Jim Edwards. BEJEWELED: The Definitive, Illustrated History Of The Most Underrated Game Ever. *Yahoo Finance* (2013). Available at: https://finance.yahoo.com/news/bejeweled-definitive-illustrated-history-most-020521265.html. (Accessed: 1st October 2018)

107. Amazon - Anticipatory Shipping. Available at: http://pdfpiw.uspto.gov/.piw?Docid=08615473. (Accessed: 25th September 2015)

108. Kirk, B. *4 Loyalty Destinations Framework.* (2015).

109. Adams, E. & Dormans, J. Gamasutra - The Designer's Notebook: Machinations, A New Way to Design Game Mechanics. (2012). Available at: http://www.gamasutra.com/view/feature/176033/the_designers_notebook_.php. (Accessed: 2nd July 2015)

INDEX

ABOUT THE AUTHOR

Andrzej is a father of two, husband (of one – because bigamy is frowned upon apparently...), reasonable guitarist, games lover, Batman nerd and Star Wars geek.

Over the years, he has had a few jobs, from web designer to learning technologist to consultant. What has always remained the same is his belief that games have much more to offer the world than just entertainment.

This led him to getting involved with gamification in his spare time. Now he is a recognised expert on the topic, writing a regular blog about gamification, keynote speaking, consulting on and designing solutions – and writing the occasional book.

Following the publication of this book, Andrzej went missing again for several weeks. This time his wife found a small ninja mask and a horse shoe with a note.

"*Even Unicorns Dream of Flying*"

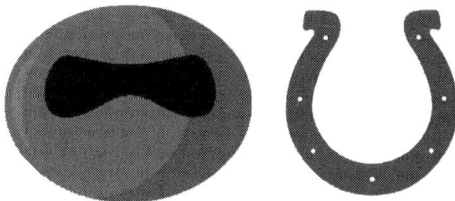

Write Me a Poem and Tweet it to @DaveRage 😊

Draw Me a Picture and tweet it to @DaveRage 😊

Printed in Poland
by Amazon Fulfillment
Poland Sp. z o.o., Wrocław